The Salt Stone

Other Books by John Woods

BOOKS

The Deaths at Paragon, Indiana. Indiana University Press, 1955. (Out-of-print.)

On the Morning of Color. Indiana, 1961. (Out-of-print.)

The Cutting Edge. Indiana, 1966. (Out-of-print.)

Keeping Out of Trouble. Indiana, 1968. (Out-of-print.)

Turning to Look Back: Poems, 1955-1970. Indiana, 1972. (Out-of-print.)

Striking the Earth. Indiana, 1976.

The Valley of Minor Animals. Dragon Gate, 1983.

SHORTER COLLECTIONS

The Knees of Widows. Broadside, Westigan Review Press, 1971. (Out-of-print.)

Alcohol. Broadside, Pilot Press, 1973. (Out-of-print.)

Bone Flicker. Juniper Press, 1973.

Thirty Years on the Force. Juniper Press, 1977.

The Salt Stone:
SELECTED POEMS

John Woods

Dragon Gate, Inc.
Seattle, Washington

9 8 7 6 5 4 3 2
First Printing

Published by Dragon Gate, Inc., 914 East Miller, Seattle, Washington 98102.

Text and cover design by Scott Walker
Type set by Irish Setter, Portland
Manufacturing by Edwards Brothers

Library of Congress Cataloging in Publication Data

Woods, John, 1926-
    The salt stone.

    Includes index.
    I. Title.
PS3545.0674S3   1985   811'.54   83-20747
ISBN 0-937872-18-0
ISBN 0-937872-19-9 (pbk.)

ACKNOWLEDGMENTS

The poems from *The Deaths at Paragon, Indiana* (1955), *On the Morning of Color* (1961), *The Cutting Edge* (1966), *Keeping Out of Trouble* (1968), *Turning to Look Back* (1972) and *Striking the Earth* (1976) appeared originally in the following periodicals: *Abraxas, Back Door, Centennial Review, Chelsea, Chicago Review, Chicago Tribune Magazine, Choice: A Magazine of Poetry and Graphics, The Critic, December, Field, Folio, Fresco, Hawaii Review, Hearse, Hierophant, Hudson Review, The Iowa Review, Kayak, Kenyon Review, Mad River Review, The Massachusetts Review, New York Quarterly, Niobe, Northwest Review, The Ohio Review, Periodical Lunch, Poetry, Poetry Northwest, Poetry NOW, Prairie Schooner, Saturday Review, Shenandoah, Skywriting, Southern Poetry Review, Sumac, Tennessee Poetry Press, Tennessee Poetry Review, Today, Western Humanities Review, Westigan Review, Windless Orchard.*

"The Night of Even Breathing" originally appeared in *Just What the Country Needs (Another Poetry Anthology)*, Wadsworth, 1971; "Light behind the Eye" appeared originally in *Westigan Review Broadsheets*, no. 3, 1971; "Alcohol" originally appeared as a pamphlet published by Pilot Press Books, 1973; and nine poems originally appeared in a chapbook, *Bone Flicker*, Northeast/Juniper Books, no. 11, 1973. The author would like to thank the editors of these publications for their hospitality to these poems, and their gracious permission to reprint them.

Author and publisher join in thanking the Indiana University Press and its editor, John Gallman, for graciously assigning to Dragon Gate, Inc. copyright on the six collections of poetry by John Woods previously published by the Indiana University Press, from which THE SALT STONE: SELECTED POEMS was compiled. We gratefully acknowledge their invaluable cooperation and support.

John Woods thanks the National Endowment for the Arts for a Writing Fellowship, which assisted his work on this book. The author would also like to thank the Division of Research and Sponsored Programs of Western Michigan University for a Research Fellowship, and the Michigan Council for the Arts for an Individual Artist's Grant, which helped in completing this book.

Finally, Dragon Gate, Inc. and the author thank the Literature Program of the National Endowment for the Arts for a grant, which greatly assisted the publication of this book.

Contents

Coming to the Salt Lick

SECTION TWO: IN THE TIME OF APPLES

I.

SECTION THREE: EVERYONE BORN IN 1926

I.

II.

III.

SECTION FOUR: THE ANCIENT COMMUNITIES

I.

II.

For Cary
1929–1983

COMING TO THE SALT LICK

They will have it.
But not in the fodder
blowing ropily green
from their yellow mouths.

Now they are coming down from the pasture,
the swinging bell, the milky blaze,
heavy, imprecise, to the acrid stone.

Why do they want it?
Why do we need it?

It is our blood, remembering its own taste,
and when we took different paths
in the forest.

Section One
The Deaths of Paragon

Part I.

On the Morning of Color
for David

On the morning of noise
our eyes kindled the hills.
Wind put the smallest leaves to our love.
With walnut hands we wrung the great coiled flight
from bitterns and other long birds
of the long morning.
Windtips blurred on the cedar
in persuasions of tilt and glide, give way
and spring back, touch wood and run home.

If we cried cold, the streams rang like bells
through tiers of oaks,
and a brown sun circled the horizon;
and weeping, trailing mufflers of coarse flame,
we chopped for fish and bombed the shelterhouse
with disappearing snow.
If we cried stop,
bright occasions held their slide
from flaming oak to shale alley.
On tip and toe the fishing birds
would weld upon their diving images.

On the morning of color,
on the morning of first-seen,
when every acorn rolled into place,
when every child seemed the final incident of poise,
when the great waters

were one small stream carrying out to river
the reflective world,
we could not sing of love or loss,
or count to thirty, holding our breath.

But now we say, God, sun,
circumstance, whatever riddles us,
send us one such morning to grow on.

A Dream of Walking

I walked in a dream of fever
in the town I grew out of,
a child, yet knowing my children.
The alleys between the old barns
yielded their tongues. The dreaming phallus,
the carved hearts, the pike's grinning jaw,
all spoke on loosening walls.

Near houses of those I loved
figures stood in their shadows,
or shadows spoke from their throats,
calling me after my father
walking a few steps before
or my children a few steps after.
I couldn't see their faces
but soon the porches were empty.

I came to the old school
whose bricks were held in a hush
of forefinger to lips, the Palmer hand
looping its fragile acrobatics
among goldenrod tablets, until graduation
cast shouting, undecipherable signatures
out into the world of falling bricks
between the two wars of father and son.

In one room, spidery with dust,
I faced the long blackboard
in whose chalk thickets
paced decimal beasts

in the bombed-out stairways
of long, parsed sentences.
My names spoke from the yellow gradebook
their unexplained absences.

I dreamed the last street,
name fallen from the corner cross,
ran, burst into the living room
of the house I grew out of.
It was empty, between families.
Strangers rose from their dinners.
It was trees before the carpenters.
Burning with fever, I ran to bed
and sank deeply into waking.

Just before Morning

The cutting bar rusts in a dark corner.
The scythe no longer gathers the moon.
A banty hen trails her seven chicks
down the dry stream,
up under the new peach trees.
The geese and the old collie
have reached an understanding
about the long grass under the arbor.
The potatoes think deeply about starch
there, in the garden,
but they'll grow up to be village idiots.

Just before the sun rolls up,
my father steps out in the wet grass,
listening four ways.
He'd be hard to surprise.

Soon the cows will complain about milk.
They'll come down, the pup
skating school figures under their hooves.
The bull on the next farm
will lean on the wire, singing.
Then the air will gather in the willow,
leveling out, pushing these thoughts,
torn pieces of New Deal posters,
through weeds and dark stones.

Flying Kites in March

It was the wind stiffening in our hands
on Cunningham's Hill told us, Spring falls past.
Nothing in our tablet tells that wind
is an old hand in leaves, wise
beyond the squeaking blackboard, and teacher
bitter and sensitive to laughter hidden in our hands.

O our hearts were lightly fastened
in this blown month, over the little town
closed by maple trees, where our thoughts tugged
a blue mile above the serried clouds.
The foliage of smoke from brick kilns
borders the scene, and we stand
tall and remarkable on the round world.

Why trees slide out on shadow
puzzles us. Why wind tangles the shirts
so they embrace on lines; why kites pull, pull,
until we kiss the distance like a face,
troubles us in the wisdom of our games.
We are ministers of touch, and bless
the shadow naves and spiring poplar.

Heavily the winds will press,
the string slacken, the kites tumble
down the sky like leaves. O is it wind
or longing pulls us down the hill,
past yards and staring mothers, past streets
with solemn names? We name them as we rush
beneath our kites: Morgan, Pike, Jefferson,

Jackson, the creamery, the fields squared
off by light and dark, the trees, the hills.

This is the end of wind, curled in a bush.
An old god of the wind will clasp us
to his tattered beard in a grove darker
than our hiding places. Pressed against
his coat, we will dance forever in leaves
fallen and falling. String, wood and paper,
whirling from the painted sky, with air
shining through the holes, surround us as we spin.

In Touch with Wind

In touch with wind turning a new leaf,
I was a bounder on the lawn, touching
all out of kilter, so very fearsome
that Spot rode his tail under the porch,
as bouncing my shoe on the hard sound,
I made the sky spit down on him.

In turncoat weather, I was the upstart
taking rain as hat and coat, shod
in several clays, wild as pod and thistle,
tuned to wind and flapping kites,
at war with cats, windows and neighborhood,
genius of the shaleslope and burred paths.

Only Grandma knew, with her cakes and dimes,
that I would pause under gliding leaves,
seized from within by halving time
that, for all my anger, takes and twins:
this for heart and this for mind.
The heart grows up, and can no longer touch.

Going Up for the Rebound

Be a leader of cheers for me,
your stopper of fast breaks,
your fall-away pumper from sidelines,
your hanger-in-space for the soft tip.
I'll press the full court of the night
to see school letters rise with your breasts,
your short skirt froth at the mouth
of tributaries to your amber thighs.

I am in all eyes, blooming with school spirits,
following your bounce and split.
Once, benched, with a knee out somewhere,
my eyes dampened like palms
as you flew and fell
three ways at once.
My center jumped.

Last night, where the car couldn't see,
I moved through a thicket of knees and elbows.
Losing and finding the ball,
I broke clear, hammered the whole length.
I flew through the basket as the gun went off,
rising like a constellation
into the scoreboard.

Barney's Sister

There's something wrong with Barney's sister
under the apple limb. That day
the door blew wide and stood her, white
and washing, in my naked eye,
I knew a sickness had her. I ran,
like from the plague, and laughed it weak
in Barney's cart behind the barn
where horses hang their shoes and collars.
Then I scattered owls with cobs.
The sun laid stalks across the floor.
I pressed my eye against the crack
to see the narrow, sunwide world.
Two roads met in a scramble patch
like what she hid behind her washrag.
Now the world is opener,
since the bathroom door blew wide
and struck me marrow deep. I stood,
white and breathing, in her eyes.
I was nakeder than she.

Once we were all straight lines
down to the salt lick by the pond.
Barney's sister wrestled me
into the cockleburs. I pinched her
where she wrinkled when she sat,
ruler thin and all wild bone.

But under the bushy sky, the apple
tree, the marrow rises; the paths
that led our hands together twist,

and I am lost in bramble, jay-
swarmed, blood-lashed.
                              Something's wrong
with Barney's sister. I pinch behind
this log and see them bathe in grass.

The moon blows wide. Something tears
in me. O all the world is ill.
Now, in their flinging legs, I see
the dead carts pass, the pyres, the blazing
streets where fever burns its halo.
There she stands in black and smears
the red name Love upon my door.

Days

1.

Long before the giant with bad breath
whistled heat through all the registers,
my grandmother would galosh at dawn
through snow to gather run-down heels
of wood and buckets of iron coal.
Pouring coal oil on the stubborn mass
she'd throw a match and jump back. Whoomph.
Each morning would begin dangerously.

Soon the Florence stove, shaped
like a Detroit coal-burning moon rocket,
would swell red-hot into the tea kettle,
as she strapped on her corset, wrapped her bun.
Then I'd leap from the featherbed
onto the ski-run linoleum for a dash
at the biscuits, gravy and coffee.
We ate like harvest hands, but the farms
had moved away, down near the river,
leaving behind red bugles of roosters,
each, in the black yards, a small, false dawn.

2.

On Halloween,
we pushed over outhouses.
Buck was famous. He fell in.
A country boy gets lost in that Chicago,
among those twisted skyscrapers.
The moon was a hole in the sky.

The catalog said *good, better, best.*
Toys and women's underthings
were the last to fall.
Nothing ever came back from those stockyards.

Brother Adams shouted hell
those Sunday mornings we stuck to the pew.
The spring broke from the hill.
Sweetcorn rose from manure.
All those old poets walked into the earth
where my mother lay.

When Buck climbed out,
the night was black with thick roots.

3.

Once we thought the gravel pit
went straight down
to the center of the earth,
where it had a red eye,
great wings of steam.

Here we knew the big girls
lay along the lapping edge
with boys our mothers didn't like.
They left a festival of pale balloons.

Deep in the black hole
sulked the whiskered catfish.
He knew something about the air
we'd have to learn.

Something deep enough.

Learning to Breathe

The street bent beneath the oaks
in light so green I rocked in a boat
all night. Outside my window, rafts
creaked around the deep tap of their anchors.
Gulls, wrens, frigate birds swung
from the rigging.
                    Walking at twelve
was gasping up from the ocean,
the green sail furling as the town
thinned into the bronze beach of wheat,
down to the fishing river, or south,
to the slamming iron hatch of the quarries.

.Then, holding my breath, I followed
my shadow into the green surging shade
of the town again, grown a little
towards amphibianhood, to dinner call,
where I ate those strange birds, the fish.

Turning to Look Back

GRANDFATHER'S VOICE

I don't even know where we came from.
So many graves stay open too long,
so many girls lie back tonight,
trying to be secret rivers in the limestone.
I want those days when nothing happens.
Not every clocktick needs a martyr.
Let my grave be a filled-in hole.
Stop shoveling me out, in the black suit
I bought for my laying-in,
to mourn your middle age for you.
Look to your own bones, John.

Tobacco-spitting, horse-shoeing, long-johned,
I lead these people out of your invention,
out of a Bible of births and deaths,
school corridors and locker rooms,
out of fumbling back seats,
into the town, trembling to rise.

We touched the first pure water,
thrusting between stones, trailing down shale,
cold and silent. Sometimes, touching water,
we know an early thing.

The women, your mother-to-be among them,
washed in the old tub, brimming for the cattle,
there, by the salt stone.
Your cousins gathered for the fire.
There we warmed, real as the day you dreamed us,

until the trees widened
into the night before your birth.

As we came down the hill at first light,
the town began from the maple valley
of the river you will call the White.
Sawdust dunes drifted into houses and barns,
where the mill turned on the bright saw
in the first sun of your eyes.
I became your grandfather,
carving a bow you couldn't draw.

I feel your eyes opening
in the dark face of your mother.
When the cord broke in the river
it leaped in a brown ridge through the willows.
Here, on this hill, I see you
letting out the kite like a far eye
over the scatter of smokehouses,
at the field's edge where the town
thins out into corncribs and fishing shacks,
old Fords driving a wood saw,
out past the cannery whistle.
Then, hand over hand, pulling it close,
struggling with the wind in it,
hugging it like the frail ribcage of a young girl;
and on this morning you made us all,
holding it to your face until the trees
stood up red through the tearing tissue.

BROTHER'S VOICE (Dead in infancy)

Just one step into air,
a step so light
it left a shadowprint
and a name vague as a touch in the throat.

And our mother wept
water as clear
as ice candelabra
and her grief was for the grief she wouldn't have.
And you will see my stone,
salt as the cattle lick
by the algaed tub
where all blood's creatures are drawn from a long graze.

Many roads start out boldly in this country,
six lanes of immaculate concrete:
this way out of the Depression.
But they soon become narrow, dodgy,
snaking around old, caulked trees
and other historical markers,
ending behind a rusting tractor
in a soil bank near Quincy.

How many Purdue graduates, tasseled and shorn,
have started West in Jaguars,
kissing the cam covers,
saying a few words over the fuel pump,
and have ended up in a Chevy Six,
with chocolate-bibbed children, spilled goldfish,
parked on the wrong side of a drive-in,
midnight, lights going brown?

19

Taking a wrong turn,
you can end up in the Thirties,
on a gravel road past oil-lit farmhouses,
then face-to-face with a swivel-jawed cow,
with a look of such staggering ignorance
you feel the presence of the meaning
of time itself. Just one step into air,
but some things come in mother's milk.

Some fill a small hole, some a large.
Much involved language has played back
through your mouth, mostly a complaint
against the one disease. A small stone
or a large, but both salt, salt.
You made me speak for the dead child in you.
I don't know whether you lived my life,
or I lived yours.

VOICES OF WOMEN

1.
Thick lashes, the night, over my eyes.
Wherever your lips touched my skin,
there was a mouth, kissing back.
My nails bit my palms,
and my throat said the oldest things I knew.
I was not there, and I was all there.
Where did I go, when my veins reached out
under the trees and the grass,
when they shrank to a hot eye
between the legs, trying to open?

And now you call me out,
deaf under my coarse skin

to lie back in the grass,
stiff in the salt of rime ice.

Let me grow old.
Beauty should pass from face to face.
A young girl walked out of me
into my daughter.
I mustn't fear her, or the days
we both can see
the black room behind the mirror.

2.

What a short world you gave me.
Spring runs in and out of Autumn,
the way you want to remember,
snow hangs in a cloud out of sight.
Hot days simmer on the back burner.
What should I do out of your eye?
Four times in bed together,
a few letters, then nothing.
When someone sings, do you know
what else that throat has wanted,
the animal in it, struggling to stand?
Four nights, some letters, and keeping,
keeping, ready to go bad,
like something dubious in Mason jars.
The basement is thick with paper,
old books and broken furniture
where I sink back
into the overstuffed bolsters of my husband.

3.

My long hair whipped your face
as I rode you home.
My buttocks clenched like a white fist
around a little of your life.

A daughter of the Gods,
the yearbook said, divinely tall
and divinely stupid. My face was a heavy rose,
and knew as much, enough, I hoped,
for your simple thirst.
Gather the roses in a swaying armful,
and cast them down, loose and sweet.
Part the inner petals and place a kiss there.
Ah, a little pollen, a coarse ornament
for a brief shaft of sunlight.
Now you find, thinking me gone,
your thighs bound with long black hair.

4.

Not so much given, as gathered,
my son, as one gathers walnuts
and opens them, staining the hands,
as boys say, with menstrual blood.
Breathed in from the scattered,
the fallen-apart, the waiting-around.
Conception is only "the field within which
the collage establishes its gesture."
Or "a whirl in the wake of joining lives."
Yes, a twig, a water bug, some embossed foam
holding together until the flat time comes.
My funeral day, you wanted to see
the Saturday Western. If I died too young,
if you have no images of me,
that will be between you and your analyst,
one of these days. There is nothing
in my will for you except a woman,
a young woman, gathering walnuts in her apron.

FATHER'S VOICE

That photo of our bivouac in 1916,
X on my tent, can't get browner.
What a parish war it seems now.
I watched you march around the barracks,
still in civvies, into another war
where I was too old to follow.

Last night, I dreamed I was there,
the canvas stiff and silver,
drain ditches running rich and brown.
Wood smoke, tart and coherent,
pushed through Company K,
and the mules shook at their tethers.
But God, John, there were only a few soldiers,
and they were old. They were old men.

GRANDFATHER'S VOICE

You came this street
before it knew its way.
As light things fall
in great March,
as rainwater finds
its own hill trail,
you came this street
before it knew its name.
Behind the light
at the front of your head,
the dark street gathers,
gathers and moves
from the first Indian
slapping out fish

to the field of stones,
out past the schoolyard.
We rose up naked
in thunderous March.
Our faces burned
like heavy medallions
under featureless skin,
and you walked down us
through dark tunnels.
We came this street
in overalls, then helmets,
now the last black coat,
from the hill of naming
to the stone names,
your brother, your father,
your mother and me,
and you behind,
paused at the gate.
Better leave us here.

Part II.

The Last Resort

I am losing. The ragged pier
goes diving in the bulging lake.
Only weather rents my skiffs.
We settle in the mud. Night
gaps the string of colored lights
around the lake. Dark reaches in.
Each day I shed a breath, closer
to shambles, my hands as empty as when
I reached for eggs upon a nest
wind untied. O I can't keep.

Once they jostled me outside
and made me dig up gin I'd made.
Inside they stamped the floor with dances.
The Class of 1925 tore down
the diving board. Bust me, I was
king of something. But we were left
behind to web and flounder, dropped.

Each day I widen like a puff
to haunt the rafters; only nearest
pains can hurt me now. The juke box
twirls its senseless colors nightly.
Nothing dances but a hat of moths
above the light. The sheriff woke me
yesterday, scratching the glass.
He'd heard that I was dead. He said
they'd dig me up like jars one day

along with buggy bones.
                    But last night
my stork came walking in the shallows,
treading his image into wheels,
fishing the moon-draped waters.
O let me widen into nothing.
I'm king of all I see. I'm king
of all the lovely visibles.

Bert in the Orchard

Mrs. Carter, glasses hanging from her eyes,
hated orchards. She rapped her buggy
past my trees. She turned me, collared
in a chalky Sunday school, away from psalms.
For I had seen her pinned beneath
the preacher on the choir stage, the moon
staining their pale thighs, staring
into their placed eyeglasses.

She led me from the preacher's words, bending
his wooden voice over the swayed parish
like a windy oak, until chandeliers leaned
from the gale, and the church hove to
in the calm collection. He read a book,
but the words were windfall, full
of troubles. O Mrs. Carter, what winds
blew me to your arms?

I had forgotten you till now. Fog
slipped up Indian Creek, bandaging
the near trees. I feel juices settling
in the fruit, and hear the quarry cough
behind Nutter's Hill. Now I remember
slow seasons in your laugh, and feel
tongues of Eve playing madness on my teeth.
Apples claimed me. I dangled, red and full.

I moved beneath the trees in fog eddies,
where the apples formed in deep green.
Here is where we lay and loved.

Fifty years, Mrs. Carter, and now I think
of you, dabbing mulch with my boot,
sensing an old chemistry the sun forces
through winding roots, embracing
with frail green the bones of something.

The Old Quarry

Under the hangs of rock, the wind is flat
as touched water. Sun blasts the limestone
until the shadows burrow under ledges.
I am here, using my bones for canes.
My eyes guard their caves. I'm deaf as stone.
It was a long wander down Devil's Slide,
tearing elbows. My cap came sailing later.
Once I pushed a drill against the face
and tamped the hole with dynamite. My head
still mumbles. Once I shivered in a hedge,
while chips of rock made bumps. The fuse was short,
and since that time I cup my ear at you.
From the cowlicked crest, I saw a shape
in all this rattle. They say that bugs once floated
over me and dropped their bones. They sank
like dust in air.
                    I, too, am an old quarry,
chased by weather, waiting for my pulse
to give me up, to strand my bones like lime.
But here my deafness doesn't matter. Birds
can tower for a life above my head.
Once the floodlights dimmed, the stonemen
rode away. Only thunder rocks the leaves.
I am here, watching the day run down.
Then, lie back, lie back, and push up stone.

The Old Man Is Dying

"I'm going to follow trees." His beard
blew like steam as he turned the corner
of the home. Spiders were swaying in on threads
across the clipped lawn. His nightgown
flapped at his red knees.

"Well now and well now, my friends." He laughed,
wetting his burning lip. At every step,
his arms flew out from his sides. The old man
stirred his bundle of bones
and crossed the road.

"My story is anger!" But no longer. Weeds
stand up between his toes. As he wavers,
crows circle his head. He sits, his gown
sifts into the weeds. The globe
of sense begins to close.

How all falls away, the breakfast thinner
on the tray. How speech withdraws
to the speaking mouth, to end there.
The loud voice failed at last,
the rant against

Silver, the ward boss, or the frozen pump
that only sighed. Or now, the damp
hands of nurses, the hoarse doctor who pinched
him and laughed, and the dissolving
world of fever.

"King's X! King's X!" As he made the sign,
he saw the faces in the window across the wide
lawn, the fingers pointing, and the grouped servants
running toward him. "They're it!" Standing,
he touched wood and was safe.

Everything Slumps at Kriner's Pier

Everything slumps at Kriner's pier.
The chevvy with its hind end up,
the rouge of rust on its doors,
slides yearly downward into weeds.
Against the claybank, a backyard clutter
dumps into the grass like dandruff.
This wake of cans and bedsprings leads
to Lincoln Road. The willows, fence
and barley move down to the water edge.
Are moving, but all is still for now,
locked in the instant of my eye.
Harold, stand up straight, my mother says.
I know the cornfield stretches
like a wick beneath the sun;
and yet, by Kriner's pier, a log
lies festering and leaking sun
through every rotten pore. All down,
sucking at the dirt, with worms
working through the shredding pulp.
Leaves that once were slick and stiff
choke the runnels. The stream digs in.

Kriner leaned too far last year.
I used to watch him through the fence,
poking windfall with his cane.
His cane was anything around.
I heard he leaned on the wind,
and it gave way. He broke hard,
pulling down the rose trellis.
Even Kriner's pier is dipping.
The fisher rocks across the planks,

thumbing the sunfish out like eyes,
to blink and blind upon the stones.

In last night's dream, I saw a fish,
an old king carp that owns the millpond.
I saw a billion years of him,
endlessly alike. Everything
that fell became his meat at last.
He has nothing but the present
to beware; and when he dies,
the thousand fingerlings he spawned
will hang, like him, beyond all time.

I'd like to crash into his pool,
boiling silt and trailing weather.
I'd poise like him, cold inside,
and take the water for my breath.
O everything slumps, and I am caught
in earth's conspiracy of air.

The Visits of My Aunt

The visits of my aunt in Martinsville
were invasions. I see the webby arbor
and the tottered shed full of kindling
and games, the willow lacing the pause
of afternoon, and townsmen rocking
under wasp shells and locust husks.
Then my aunt's car would startle dogs
to ragged challenges as she blew her horn
down Grant Street. Puffing out onto the yard
with a moustache and blue-wet dress,
she hugged me breathless. Her car door
slammed down birds from the carved maple.
The keepsakes would jump when she sat:
the plaster horse and carnival cane,
the one ashtray kept for her flourishes.
Our latest uncle tugged the creases
in his pants and face, and tapped his watch.
Summer ventured in her voice.
That rusting crankcase filled with rain,
half-hidden in the weeds, held no
more rainbow than she stroked from air.
The steaming dump up Lincoln Road,
with rats and springs, held no more
oddness than her pocketbook
to trick us with. While she spoke
clouds held their rain, and August
lay like lambs beneath her spell.
The piano repeated, deep in its harps,
her essential hum.
         When she died
under the glass tent, I grew into an answer:

life, as well as death, can last forever.
There is a heaven of things: car doors,
uncles, the ashtray from the Exposition.
But as she withered in the tilted bed,
I came with the first frost to another meaning:
something of brown leaves, withered grapes,
the ganged birds exploding from the oak;
that someday the easy wind would knot,
and I'd be helpless in the grip of days.

The Deaf Man

That splintered day, that week of railing winds
and hard water, that month of eiderdown,
his world drew back, past the hanging barn
he read stars through, further than the lake
with its bleach of sand, the waters ironing the grass,
until he heard nothing but his booming head.
The wind read his lips, and he saw such singing
as there was, shocked before him like the winter wheat.

Wet, stacked landscapes steamed in the morning
when only the sky rang blue. Behind his head
the birds thundered, the wormy oaks sang madrigals.
Now his wife shrilled to her ears the spars of clutter
and second choices, and her anchor sparked
on the stony hills and armored corn.

But he grew around her in such a poise
he seemed a millglass sterned around a reed.
As snow floured the panblack hills, love returned,
a channel swimmer in a spray of silence, where
in snow geese evenings they floated
in the featherbed. Then, urged beside her
in an Australian crawl, he sang of love Down Under.

The Totem Man

I built my totem near the quarry stone
below the field of wind, the rattling corn,
the millwheel walking down the waterfall.
I shaped a man, my totem animal,
from branches, murky soil and pasture dung
and set my breath rebounding in his chest.
From a bird stoned red beneath an elm,
I took a wing for tongue, to stride his breath
and praise our name. I knew October leaves
would burn like martyr's fire around his feet,
that bees would cloud his belly with a hive.
At last, I blessed him with the elements:
with flame so he might flare venereally,
with tears to blur the hating world, with breath
for divination of the song, and with clays
for we are near the edge of moulder always.

I betrayed my totem man a thousand days.
I led him lost by his shaken hand.
By the hollow of his heart, I showed him
all the seasons of the human world.
Up there, the field is dense with wind and rain.
Shacksmoke races through the maple trees.
The bloody rabbit swings at the hunter's belt.

I burn my totem near the quarry stone.
Flame forks like blood in his thicket wrist.
He utters smoke. O all the elements are loose.
The world breaks in from the rasping field

where the scareman totters in the aisles of corn.
Was he my totem? Now the wind springs back
into my throat. Twigs lie crossed where he fell,
empty of love. The May woods burn with Autumn.
A fist of birds assaults the yellow maples.

Birth Day

I rose from unusual water, crying
there is a wound that never heals, a mannafield
    as wide as lap
where I lie in the throbbing dark, crying
    leave me in the black
        on this loveliest of maps,
           sealed
from dawn that would end my lying.

I hurried to the indolent willow
where the sun made honey on the waspy pool.
    I never knew
why the bank grew warm, the willow
    lashed and blew,
        dipped in the lucid
        pool,
or what makes growing out of fallow.

That summer, in the canal, playing
with round stones bent by water, tarry gravel
    and hiding crawdads,
I sensed the prying waters playing
    papa to fish,
        sliding in the rushy
        hovel,
kissing the sleepy seed to daying.

I walked with Alice through the glass.
I felt her hand squeeze tighter as we entered light.
    But why she turned

and took me to her bed, no magic glass
can merge the learned
and the lost into an answer.
O child,
look, the mirror closes as we pass.

The Log of the Ark

Now, Noah said, "These are the rules
you creatures must obey:
Keep your hatches firmly closed,
no smoking in the hay.

"Elephants, restrain yourselves,
we've room for only two.
Such exercise would spring our strakes
and dunk us in the blue.

"The latrine detail will form a line.
Whoever designed this raft
forgot that we would soon go down
if all went pushing aft.

"No dice, no dancing, no unions, please.
Take care with whom you dine.
The brotherhood of animals
is only party line."

So Noah lectured to the beasts
until his voice grew thin;
Man before the Innocents,
telling how to sin.

He felt the furnace of their breath;
their eyes were burning near.
Then the tiger raised his paw
and sprang his sabers clear:

"Man, we are custodians
of all the sparks of life.
Now take your notes and podium
and lecture to your wife.

"Your whale oil lamps have guttered
in the temples of your pride,
and no one wears my gaudy coat
above the midnight tide."

Noah threw his sounding line
but pulled up wet laundry.
"We are the last of life," he cried,
"above the groaning sea.

"We are the last alive," he prayed,
"beneath the bursting sky."
"You are the last that live," he heard,
"in all the galaxy."

And so he climbed the creaking mast
to where the yardarm crossed;
and Noah, in his high lookout,
played solitaire, and lost.

Near Carter's Mill

By walked-along water, the trees hang fire.
The roundhouse wind gives blood to my cheek.
In loved-down grass, by nesting air,
the hare lies gathered, tight and quick.
And near the shalebed, rundown stream,
the millwheel stands in the spraying flume.

From whistle-far town beyond the wheel
where a Sunday sky, ringing with clouds,
holds dusty horizons of October hills,
I fled this morning the well-drawn words
of the preacher with his turning tongue
to the trembling wheel where racewaters lunge.

Under the quiet millstone reels
the browbeaten hill in an autumn rain,
the scored gulleys floundering downhill,
the bent-tined lightning, and the veins
of thunder cracking the roiling ore.
The millstone trembles on the leafdrift floor.

When walked-alone water, by the falling trees,
says, This is your book with a windy page,
where the wet thumb counts and the wet eye grieves,
then the deep heart thunders against the age.
By overboard water, I strike as stone.
I blow the grist and seize the grain.

O faraway town with your prince and poor,
I stand six miles up Lincoln Road
where time held close, while the world went over
to the elbowing town where wheels go mad,
where the factories spew by the granary,
with bread for you, but none for me.

The Room

I know this room
and this man in it.
Turned from his country,
his children curse him,
or worse can't remember
their days among roses,
the dog in a circle
and his eldest in it.

This room is for rent,
torn by the passage
of men from the stations.
Though some met their wives,
their nights among children,
he leaves his key
with a man at the desk,
goes out for some chili,
night upon night.

I know this room now,
rocked by the elevated,
the telephone thinking
of how to begin.
His hand on his eyes
reddens the light.
He turns in his life
on a knuckle of ice.

The Girl Who Had Borne Too Much

That girl has borne too much,
there, in her locked bed.
We need to see the caul flaming,
the drooled lip, ancestral greed
stamping its old medallion
on the childish brow, something
dragging a swollen foot
at the edge of our shadows.

But whatever walks her night corridors,
its hair burning, does not lie
in her arms. Now her face is smoothed
back to childhood.
                        Child, and whoever
wears your young body in the bad nights,
we know that the whore
may breathe sweet milk,
and a lean christ lie back at ease
in the fat-rinded murderer.

Uncle

The foxred sun went diving into the hill.
Dark hunkered near the grinding wheel.
We sat against the shed and on the wall.
Inside, the woman rumped and fried, beetles
racked against the screen, a wasp circled
its crackwebbed providence. The night perked
with fugal crickets. Coffee chugged black.

The parlor, where uncle rocked, reeks
with flowers he never knew. Weeds
bloodied his pruning hook. Red seeds
cast from his winding scythe bled
in his beard, where the colors of raked sod
now on the silk, the polished coffinwood,
pour from his rouged face their watershed.

Thin as Gideon paper, his skin glows
over white twisted knuckles, the slab cheese
of yellow palm, the horned facets of fused
glass nails: the weapons in his tomb.
Never will the hillside break again, the juice
of chopped milkweed bleed pearl, the fruit
spread its seed beneath his hobbed boot.

We die into our dinner. Wine bleeds
in our mouths, bones leap from the meat
and fall to the hounds beneath the trencherwood.
Painfully we glut with heavy food,
and whittle from the monument of cheese.
Our mouths are empty, our eyes are dead
as from the coffin loaf we break with bread.

The Deaths of Paragon

1. SANDRA, THE WAITRESS
Sun streaked the coffee urn
and wrote AL'S LUNCH across the cups.
I saw no harm in summer then,
and held against the scorching sun
a spring, touching the deepest earth,
that trickled in the bearded tub
behind the store. But nothing holds
when fire levels on the frying concrete.
Thermometer said *Go easy, girl.*
Dodge trouble. And so I fed
the truckers, watching the tube of coffee
twitch along the urn, the street
repeat itself across the mirror.
I washed an egg beneath the tap.

Then, too sudden for the mind,
the car came rolling, spraying parts
and boys across the road outside.
He came, and comes forever, sliding
headfirst into the curb.
The egg broke beneath my hand.
O this to say: His arm was bent
behind his back. Dust and leaves
crawled down the gutter.
O this to hope: Someday his eyes
will close upon my dream.

2. GOSS, THE AMBULANCE DRIVER
My head spins in the siren
but I hold the road. Muscles

keep the old shapes. When oaks
are ripped by lightning, tip to root,
does sap spring out until the tree
hangs flat as an inner tube
from junkyard fences? Dr. Sweet,
this siren calls *I am the cross
your training binds you to.*
But hear, one behind is crucified
on a steering wheel, and bleeds
his heart away. Sew on him
a year, and he will lie unbuckled.
The highway whips my face,
and all my riders are emptying
behind me.

        O this to say:
lives are balloons. When the moorings
drop, the wind takes you sailing.
Someday the wind goes slack, and they
come spinning like my passengers.

    3. CHAUNCEY, THE JUNK MAN
Scatter me, wind. I am the king
of bang and rattle, of fall apart
and rust in weeds. I am where
things wobble off to. My offerings
sail from back stoops: wires
distracted into sparks, handles
that give you pains, broken holders.
When I am mayor, every matron
will come unglued and hit the spot
with all her joints aglow.
But I can coax a shape in anything,
make it stick and tend and solder.

O this to say: today I dragged
a mash of wheels and sparking sides
into my shed. I cluttered ledges
and festooned rafters. But when
I gathered shape into my brain,
I cowered under fenders, reeling.
The shape was fall and spin and blast.
The shape was death. I let it go.

4. Doctor Sweet

Yesterday I fished for bass,
but now I fish for breath in bones
clasped as bottom roots. The pulse
nibbled like a chub but got away.
All five of you are dead.
Light beaks my eyes, and edges
my knives with fire. Though I link
you by my chart, you'll dangle empty.
Even Chauncey, with his shed of parts,
can never make you run. I know
he'll tow your flattened car away
and hang its pieces from his roof
like sausages and collarbones.
He'd bandage you with earth.
I know those visitors below.
Because you left them yet to be,
they come to lynch you with their tears.

Now I give you to their hands
for burial in summer earth.
O this to hope: that you will never
wake upon an empty world,
and cry for love, and hear no answer.

Part III.

Mental Institution

Birds went all day, and dust walked the path
under the iron gate. I touched a flower
but it flew away. I picked up grass
but the wind hooked it.
A woman was kind so she could watch.

Yesterday, a bird flew in the ward
and went crazy, trying to light on nothing,
peeping and dropping feathers.
Wind was lost in his wings. We knew,
but Nurse was scared.

Doctor said he'd cure me, one way or another.
But until the bird learns the sky has shrunk,
and nests in light bulbs, I'll keep
behind my eyes and tightening skull.
O let the doctors find where birds go
in my head, clutching for roosts; and see,
in the cage I wear, there's no way out
but in, and there my madness beats its wings.

Bone Flicker

Some bones announce we are cruising at 580 mph.
Some bones look in to see if some bones left the key.
Bones are getting married tonight.
Others find a wet spring bad for the patio business.
Bones all over the Kona Coast.
Bones lecturing to bones *on* bones.

Around bones, a haze,
a kind of flicker,
talking in a wet, smacking way
about scratching, mostly,
an itch, an itchy bone,
wanting out.

The Hate

My plant and I live together.
You know how they grow, taking the chandelier
one day, greening all light
through the steamed windows. At night, its fronds
come to my lap.
                 So this is love.
I was a patron of the penny arcade
with its postcards and naked maybe's
scooting by too fast. I had a girl,
but you know what she did. Before Plant,
I call those days.
                 When you have your plant
you need nothing. The air thickens with oxygen.
You reel all over. Its roots are with you.
O and when it blossoms that one time,
blood and smoke are gathered in your arms.
As the neighbors cluster at your door,
you wear your wreath, black as the wick of a vein,
roots going all ways inward.

Insurrection in the Seed

Insurrection in the seed
inched me from sleep. With rivers at my waist
I heard battles breaking in the earth,
    stems bend, and windy knives turn
blood out on the strategic road.
    Civility could not last.

As the night turned smally
in snarled oaks, and an owl blinking,
noise grouped a pulsing mile
    from groping sense. My household fell,
a home divided into wholly
    flame and under, sun and sinking.

Nine months' desperate news
from front lines proclaimed a crisis in the soil.
Dynamos pulsed in the blacked-out mill;
    like storks, the bombers trailed
high air. The armies swept their choice
    from home, though home was ill.

With the river crossed,
the last trench bridged, I came to terms with day.
Domains of sleep passed from my hands;
    my house was searched and banned.
I spun the enemy's banner as the General passed.
    And I swore before authority to hate.

Outcome and Downfall

The world is burning. Rust
flickers in the harrow.
The long-dividing dust
simmers in the marrow.
And girls will dazzle by
with flame at breast and thigh.

A porch swing rides the flood
The mind goes under thrice
in the millrace of the blood,
or thickens into ice.
Whatever men devise
the corporeal denies.

The wind that blows my tongue
until I think I sing,
in every tree has sung,
and will sing, everything.
Wind blows through my bones.
Which is the one that moans?

The gods that blessed the earth
have long been out of town.
Though dirt invented birth,
the signposts still point down.
This mustering of grief
still totters with the leaf.

To the Waiters for Miracles

You will not gather pears again in blue aprons,
nor poach the buff deer.
There are no kings worth dying for.
Nor will you see the black loam turned,
the wind come back and wheel again
its green springing.

No luck will save you, nor faith
in a letterhead. No benefactor shall name you heir.
For names shall die, and no horseman
suddenly visible, nor nonstop serum,
nor bread from stone
shall stop the fall of stone.

No woman again, no, not ever,
her hour come upon her, shall lie in the beak
of God, deaf in the artillery
of wings, and make of her own blood and milk
a thin bearer of flesh for more or less
than our skin's sake.

Nor you, singer, worn by song to the quick
of your throat, nor you, poet,
riding the undulant wave of language
near coasts where man in the dark
fights your ancient war in chaos
and animal cries. . . .

Told, Then Told Again

Told, then told again, by night,
in rain blurring the fathom lights
and smoothing the palm-and-knuckled bay.
Told by night when eyelids shape
a microverse of flares, pinwheels and shooting dust.
Told by the crossed trees and the river,
changing its place with rain, and the salts
of seven white-rimmed and fishfull seas.
Told by the scrabbling poor in the wet shards of the city,
by lands-end, precipice, parapet and afterlife, told:

Pray to bread, that it still rise,
waxed against the vein of dissolution.
Pray to culture, that bread may live beyond its day of yeast.
Pray to money, that it sweeten the miser in his last vault.
(And how, in its dispensation, like the early death of leaves.)
Pray to animals, O Ignorant, for they may judge us yet.
Pray to all the gods, for they are what we mean by images.
To wind, for it moves the woodsmoke across the willow-brake.
To rain, for the burning web of streetlights in the black tree.
To dung, for it completes the cadence which began with seed.
And pray to fire for what we learn in ashes.

And I was told this in the pelting season,
in dry grass, by all the torn, shed, pawned
attributes of the solid world. Nothing I was born with
is worth throwing away.

Lights Out

Easy enough, the eyes' delighting.
The corrupt are often beautiful,
what else for?
              The hand is not moral,
nor is food the ultimate weapon.
Nor is bed, where two fine pelts
stretch on one another:
appetite is skin size.

What a border! where we stall
at the electric fence of senses,
reaching, in flare light, to know
some other immaculate compound.

But, lights out, we fall back from our eyes,
back from the coast.
              This country
is ready to be ruled, the interior
sweet with its mines, tribes, headwaters.

This is no place to be lost in:
you, and you, your enemy.

Crashes

Those that come in hard
through marsh grass and cypress
at the end of runways, shedding
wing panels, wire and fluid.
Those who lose it in rain
down mountain trails
and catch it briefly until
the rear end comes around
and the steering wheel
bucks and strikes.
Those whose money turns on them
and explodes in their wallets
when the grain suppurates
in the dock strike, who are lost
in green leaves and falling columns.
Those whose veins lock them
in one cold side of their brain,
one crying corner of a mouth
saying half the world of riches,
one eye red on the cheekbone.

Outburst from a Little Face

He is crying there near the toilet.
Mother not enough.
Father gone into the roof altitudes.
Tired of seeing his little face
warped in shoe leather.
Afraid of the menstrual towels,
the bicker and shouting
of the storming ceiling.

Let me out of this dwarf.
I want my full voice.
I don't want to be the submarine
riding the pillow behind the sofa.
I want this thing between my legs
to hang heavy and gnarled as
the steaming grain of the table leg.

I'm tired of sitting on my lap
to reach the cereal.

The Murder

Papers, leaves held the porch.
The mailbox bloomed. One wasp, in armor,
chinned into his stone hut.
Inside, I lay with my black wound,
face down, with one arm and leg
swimming from the couch. The radio praised.

Inspector, there are no clues here.
Gather wild flowers rather than motives,
tireprints, notes, the circled date.
Measure your own wound if you must.
Arrest the radio, it knows something.
Life is its own blunt instrument.

Auction Day

Love as you must in the library.
I've never been wet-thumbed or pored over.
Never before or enough, as the books
open on their weak spines. Stories
that should face the wall. Shame
in dust jackets.

      The cows fill with milk. The wet hay
      smoulders. There are webs in the grass.
      Bones in the drowned coffins. High geese
      draw a ragged bow.

Let there be something in the water, please, for I
am an old coach. Some trace of a fallen star,
so boys will grow out of their socks, caps,
out of their minds. Send them down the shale
from the hill farms. I'll untangle their hair
from the nets.

      Let Johnny come back from Camp Atterbury.
      Let the saved-in-Jesus take my hand.
      Let the river sleep near the low corn.
      Let the porch swing innocently squeak.

Crime sleeps in this half pint. I'm lost
under the bleachers again, the only cop
in town. Ten Four, I ask. Ten Four, I answer.
Someone in a stolen car loves me, Drunk-at-Law
in the jailblock of my ribs.

Well it's Old Long John.
He's a long time gone.
Like a turkey through the corn,
With his long clothes on.

It's bad to be blue, but worst
to be nasally blue. Half the women
in the Hills of Adenoids are breaking up
housekeeping. The other half are
breaking up furniture.

O Baby, why does you treat me
like a dog? I got a short leash
and a low roof and a empty bowl
and I scratch this on the sunburst
chest of an old guitar.

Ever since I met your daugh-ter
I've had trouble passing wa-ter
Footprints on the dashboard upside down.

Depression glass, handmade barrels,
genuine oil paintings, cultivators,
a Massey-Ferguson tractor, '48 Ford
made into a pickup, milk cans,
mule harness, ice picks, 30 bales
of hay, crutches, featherbed,
an aunt who rocks forever, an uncle
who thinks he's going to live
with Billy in Florida.

Joe "Sonny" Gridley,
Auctioneer

Section Two
In the Time of Apples

Part I.

The Touch

When I touch your body
my hand takes your whole shape.
Even I am beautiful
one close minute.

It is seeing
the sculpture in the stone.
It is knowing in perfect greenness
where kneeling on the earth
would make it
flower.

The Hill Is Born in Fire

The hill is born in fire
again, the windthrown
birds thicken the trees
until the trees are singing
and the hill is worn by fire.

Again the dogs are hunting
in the wet bark of the wood.
Treetops break into smoke
as the windfed birds are tossed
from the dogs and hunting fire.

The hill hides under wings
where the night-jarred birds sing
until the hill is singing,
and a dog hunts his lost bark
in the wet hide of the hill.

O we sang, two in the bush,
that a bird in the hand
of the four-tined wind flew
beneath our forking hide
on the firetorn hill again.

Water, Still Water

Water,
still water,
stop the leaf
in the flawed pool,
until the wreath
above the dropped
stone lies
still.
    Water,
still water,
hold our love
though our faces fade
into shore weeds,
with white birds,
and bright
leaves.

Come to Me and Singing

Come to me and singing
in the risks of love.
On this sure morning,
streets run to the lights,
the clock winds my pulse.
Down the trees, shadows
make a night, and night
is our nakedness.
There are woods, parks,
wild as the days before
the accidental cities,
the only clock,
rime ice on water.

There are wild places in our lives
where we may be possible.
My nerves rise to the skin
and my skin takes the world.
Though the trees seethe with fire
in the deep iris of your eye,
come to the risks of love,
come to me and singing.

Maine Scene

Thin in the milkweed,
wet by the fishery,
tall by the linden,
the wind and the windcock
turn on the season.

Robins had warned me
music can tighten,
thinner and harder,
wind in the basswood
sung below hearing.

What is the reason?
White in the bindweed.
What is the reason?
Brown in the fairway.
What is the reason?

The axe in the heartwood
two ridges over
is seen before hearing,
heard before falling
and falls out of living.

That is the reason
the true song is native,
stays out the winter.
The pond ice will loosen
and kingfishers come.

Again the Quiet Night

Again the quiet night.
The alderbush is quick with birds.
Again the vegetal beast called countryside
is poised on stem and tendril.
Again the green is pressing
on closed shades, on moth-drumming screens
of simmering cabins.
Again the lovers brim with sweetness
where they are closed
in the black
of the green
of the night.

Happily because April

Happily because April wore
your flashing pelt, I sing
this praise of everything:
water, sycamore,
the breathing of the wine
across your lips to mine.

Deeply as the grass
was taught by comb in hair
to undulate in air,
our passions sift and pass,
and in your eyes, the wind
and water whorl and blend.

But yellow takes the oak.
And autumn takes the heart.
Love and counterpart
fall away in smoke.
I celebrate the stone,
the limits of the bone.

In the Full of Love

In the full of love,
when the throat is too rich to speak,
in the stopped and waiting time
of the fountain's blossom,
we could feel, out night windows,
the plaited rootworld, collations of leaves,
the gravid belly of the moon.
One bird could say
out of the airy mansions
this is my green room
where I fall from egg to bone
in one feathered arc.
Not the trembling time
in the first night hall
when we gave our fears
and stiff prides away.
Not the shambled end
when we shrank in each other's eyes.
But the full time
that seemed the death of time,
as over the flick and tantrum of meadowgrass
we set our rich aspic.

How So Lovely Walks the Wind

How so lovely walks the wind
beside the chafing waterwheel.
Soon the sliding stream will rind
and winds will hollow at the mill.

Now that wind will have its way
I take my lovely girl in hand
deep in shaken grass, and lay
her back into the shape of wind.

How so deeply will we lie
when all the greenery burns low
that wind will roll its caissons by
a mound of summer in the snow.

Every Barley Tongue Is Loose

Every barley tongue is loose.
Geese lord it over the grass.
   Tightened to the meadow, sun
strikes no colors but gray and dun.

Hard by the wheat, the water curds.
October's sky goes blind with birds.
   Now we see through the thorny hedge
even the lightest wind is edged.

Our summer love was touch and go.
But when the sky goes blind with snow,
   within our hearts we'll tend a storm.
Between our hands we'll keep love warm.

The Elements

How bitterly I fell from sense
to take my breathing through her hair.
She bedded with the elements:
water, fire, earth and air.

We drowned the world of innocence.
From our husks no son or daughter
rises from the elements:
fire, air, earth and water.

I saw us through a shrinking lens;
down we crumpled into birth
and scattered to the elements:
air, water, fire and earth.

Let love be that intelligence
that rises from the funeral pyre
to sing a song of elements:
earth, water, air and fire.

Lie Closed, My Lately Loved

Lie closed, my lately loved, in the far bed
at the foot of the moon, barred by sash and shade.
Now your eyes are shells adrift in shadow.
Under the furled sheets, the long sloop
of your body swings about
the anchor of a dream. The dark applause
of leaves wakes in the wind
the ear makes when it hears no wind.
The sapling bows against the wall
in the footlight of the moon.

One hour away from sweating animals,
afraid to wake the children or themselves,
we're locked apart, though something of your shape
still molds my hand. I breathe you still.

A heavy stallion rumbles in the straw,
stud for all the trembling mares.
Around his yellow mouth hang crumbs of flowers.

The Young Girl Speaks

Narcissus, love me, turn your eye
from water and watch me as I pass.
Why kneel and watch the whirling sky
as I do in the looking-glass?

I find you rapt in tousled water,
your world that point where stare meets stare.
You kiss yourself like any daughter
who thinks her mirror is aware.

Where the flattened waters turn
the sky against the sky, you stand
and love that loving face that yearns
to throw itself upon the land.

Where the flurried waters fan,
your corrugated image blows.
But waterbirth has given man
the need to enter where he rose,

where nothing moves, and nothing will
if you walk downward through that floor.
Narcissus, lie upon my sill.
I am the water. I am the door.

Windfall

when she was ripe
she wore barley and shadow
and sang down the wet tunnel
of the cistern

when she was ripe
she held her breasts up
to the thin drizzle
of the falling month

and young runners
circled her fences leaving
poems tied with vine
in her trellis

the country was dying again
the wheat bleached away
leaf combers
her body was a mouth

the oil drum boomed
under the gutters and she laid
lilac in her long clothes
and turned the light off
in her birth room

The Woman, Opened by Loving

She lies as the earth, where mountains
gather, where black rivers
piston through lime, knees apart,
eyes half closed.
She slips almost under.
Now to touch her is to run, all hands,
through wet landscape, to have air
fall through you.

She takes you in her
as you came from her,
riding to light,
standing to pain, as first trees
hardened to species, the taloned rose.
At the dark arch,
you pressed wet leaves
to the wounds of passage,
the rift blood of exodus.

The cradle of her mouth
rocks your tongue, though it cries
the words before words;
and in the gnarled wood of her groin
you are chosen by your choice
to walk the Theban road
on the dark side of your brain,
to kill, then love,
whom you should have loved and killed.

When she takes your seed
you are the god of spring again,
casting two-handed

down the broken, raining field.
As you flower to one another,
the orchards thunder with falling fruit.

It was a priest of weather
wrestled your bodies down
into the windfall winesaps
until the polar season
walked from your twined loins
to populate the earth.

Woman, opened by loving,
you are to be told upon,
before poems, when the throat
ached to say, truth before truth,
and the soil arched back to utter.
You are Eden again,
and all things are possible.

Part II.

In My Darkest Age

In my darkest age
I loved your medieval
lips that dripped with gall
and honey in their rage.
I hung upon their feast
and gorged like any beast.

In our duel of tongues
your kisses let out blood.
Beneath your falcon's hood
I urged such tender songs
that, gentled by such pap,
you fed me from your lap.

But last night in your cell
I heard the shadows speak
that others, drawn and weak,
had swung within your bell
and made the armor boom
across the freezing room.

I lie this lonely hour
and hold you, ignorance.
I know what renaissance
is knocking at the tower.
But when the towers spill,
I'll swing, your clapper still.

Friend, of Distances

What is your living, friend
   of distances, in the room
you illumine, where my
yesterday's weather hums
   on your phone?
   Woman with child
   and oleander, time
to say I remember
more than your red bush,
   Fox! August, and the
asters are stupid, but
   their fuses are lit.
   The word is out
among crawlers that apples
   forge the sugar chains.
   This botany means that
love need not answer letters
for all is known to
   the knowers, friend of distances,
redtailed hawk who
reads the grass tremor
   at eye's end, tell
   me your living.
You once told me your tremor
   in bed, in the bed
   below the bed, when
you sighed time's thunder
   in my ear,
   deeply ancient
so that street names
flew and the town
   was lost in its state,

and the servers
of processes, the faces
that would frown
us home, flattened
into snapshots in purse
and wallet, when oleander
veined the room.
    August, now, and the slow
    fuse burns along my hands,
and the asters open
their dim flames, your gifts
    as I remember you
    in them, friend of distances,
what is your living?

To the Young Woman

All on a day
the spring burned its light attributes
the willow gestured in its ground

So might the young woman
in whose blank nights the wall flowers urged
where five rivers webbed
across the streetlit ceiling
hug to her breast the sword of spring
flashing four ways at the garden clock

So might the young woman
at whose sandy waist the lion purrs and rolls
in whose tan flank
the bones lie sleeping
draw with her breath a jungle of tawny dandelions
and swallow through pale cheek
the dangerous rose
hair, hide and tallow
bellow and red tooth

So might the young woman
paused at the green stone and green spray
a prisoner of archery
find in the elbow of barberry
the twists and tonsure of life
and sing of it so purely
the thickets would be combed

Loss

These, the artifacts of loss:
milk souring into layers,
ingots of bread upon the table,
no one, no one on the stairs.

I see my face in mirrors, note
the sadness of a failing race.
Last of Lovers, song in mouth,
seeks the meaning in his face.

I count the tapdrip of the days
which fall like leaves from the wall.
I turn to the phonograph and hear
the artist crying for us all.

The cat that no one quite puts out
is scratching at the kitchen floor.
High tides rose the night you left.
You smiled a little at the door.

When the tide drew back, it left
a conch shell on the steps; and daft
I took to bed with this device
where, close against my ear, you laughed.

Gradually the Summer Leaves

Gradually the summer leaves
the joints and apertures, treefork
and knotted grass, the hare's breath
runnel in the thinning park.

The sun is not itself in the fountain.
Crimson smarts in the oak. Birds
as thick as leaves fall southward
across the fields, the heavy herds.

Across the trellis, trumpet vines
revise their purple passages.
The bruised pear darkens, rain
seethes in the crisp hedges.

And what to say, my summer girl?
Having had its lark, the lark
flies on. All month long we'll hear
the snow men gather in the park.

The Restless Solomon

When, in a dream of loving, Solomon
kicks his furs, the wind sifts his beard
like kisses lying in the tongues of women.
His eyes and nostrils flare. With sword upreared,
he bursts from bed, and candles dodge his wake.

He halts between his harem and his gourd
of ink. His notebooks and his women shake,
for he is mighty with both pen and sword.
He thinks: "There is a girl who keeps
the vineyard, who has kept her own
from winestained kings. Although my harem weeps,
I'll find a vineyard we can plant alone."

He stirs his wives and beats upon their gongs,
and there retires to write his *Song of Songs*.

Verges

"The edge is what I have."
Roethke

1.

The red truck sifts into the weeds.
I think of my pistons often,
when I was a distributor of sparks.
I was warned to regulate my voltage
in the years of FDR.
Sweetly my shocks were steady
and my springs arched clearly.
I will not present you with my rear end.
When my betters swallowed goldfish,
I was geared for the hard inch uphill
and my brake drums glowed
after the fast descent.
Rust has its shape, its smoulder,
steel on its way to ore,
my waiting body, banking
its fires.

2.

It will never be enough
to stand at the verge and cry:
I will not step away,
I will not step back.
The flood is brewing in the parlor,
the roof is dealing all the deck.
I pause with my candle stub
on the floating, flying stairs.
Behind me a thousand candles
glow down to the furnace room.
Above me a thousand candles
flash outward to the sky.
Down there my mother is rocking,

as the water lifts her skirt.
Father is on the silo,
waving an American flag.
Come and get me, sonny,
and *Come back into the firm.*
Three tears for her milky breast.
An erection for your flag.
But I must be flying off.
Here I come, Icarus, baby.

3.

I take this cadence from a man named Roethke.
I take it and I keep it.
For it is the essence of Theodore
that the eye carry the print of stems
long after one has fallen,
stare-first, into the hedge.
The hedge is the boundary
between my neighbor, who does not drink,
and the happy open of gin.
Up she goes, like a kite with a tail of bras.
Her breasts are full of noble gases,
my neighbor's wife, who does not drink,
and the jinn rises from the cup
like the foliage of juniper
crossing my eyes with hedges.
For Roethke crossed the hedge
into the kingdom of weeds,
coarse king of the delicate.

4.

Strange barking in the west field,
the red field, where the grain
dies a night before the harvest.
A black barking where the sun
falls apart in thickets.

My throat aches in their voice,
their single weariness, like one dog
with three snowgrizzled heads.

Sometimes the stars make a sound,
a tremor of fine sword steel,
and under it, like a drum's memory,
the bass silence of a struck stone.
Then the house creaks, like a ship
heeled in the long trades of time.
Each joint sings that the carpenter
left off-rhymes in his wooden lyre.
I hear my silence in these night sounds.
Surely I will die in this black room.
Lean down, coroner, for my last words.
Then,
in a far room,
my wife sings a sweet catch.
Such human breaking in me.
In all this gathering blackness,
a small lamp is lit
and the night blazes.

1945-1965: *To My Student*

Not knowing what to wear for the occasion,
she put on too much lipstick
and a rhythm section of cheap bracelets.
She bathed for an hour.

She was picked up before the skating rink
by a soldier on leave from Texas.
Spirited away from the bar,
she lay back, dim-eyed, in the Hilltop Motel,
parting like a new loaf.

Beneath her tart's clothes,
she was nearly pure.
Beneath her purity, the urgency
which now lifts her knee to the executive
at the Country Club dance.

Beneath it all, the dark, rented room
where you were conceived, my student,
to whom such wars can never be explained.

Suburban Note

Give me an old practitioner
who wears a dark device
to turn my middle inside out
and run my marrows ice.

We love our women by the book
with twenty-three positions:
1) Put it there, 2) Wind it up,
3) See Table Nine for visions.

Send me a wild adventuress
who forgets to wind the clock,
who locks me in an iron safe
then tampers with the lock.

Send me that sweet inventoress
who forgets to wrap the bread,
who rings the changes with her toes
upon the brass bedstead,

who forgets to set the thermostat,
and wears a feather boa,
who rides the chaste and glacial sheets,
a rumbling Krakatoa.

Now the Singing Is Over

Now the singing is over,
and that woman has gone
to lie in a new coat of arms,
on a white field, rampant.
I had not said my piece
about the life of the skin
of her inner thigh, or the line
that darkly drew to the demitasse
of her navel.

There I became
all tongue and taste, while the night
swayed with candles. The breathing,
the crying out, the warm mouth
of love under the willow hair.

She is gone from the high window.
Another spills the wine of her body.
Another's cigarette brings to light
the wet silk of her trembling shoulders.

There was no war to make
a terrible dignity of our parting.
Nor were we separated by the curse
of a mad woman in the tower,
or a secret wound from Spain.

The kitchen rose between us.
The toaster strained to become a refrigerator;

the living room, a nursery. All the ads
said *buy, become,* and *we love you more.*

She goes to a new bed
where the man who will fill her
with babies sits, looking sadly
at his wedding shoes,
and his cuff of rice.

In the Time of Apples

In the time of apples
love turns away again.
Your face has closed a door.
As green light darkens
my eye forgets to know.
My voice has taken root
where the lights are out.

Trees leap up thinner
and fall before my eyes.
My fingers know as much
as they will ever know
except that thing the orchard
leans at last to say.

I forget already
the woman of your face.
The hammer of the fruit
falls through your voice.
Here on this window ledge
something you owned goes strange.

I will not say that autumn
explains this apple time.
No one owns an orchard
since Adam loved the world
enough to let it go.

The Woman Who Is One Woman

The woman who is one woman
remembers the egg time, the time
of the blind fish.
               She remembers
herself as one, long body
rising from the beginning.

But the woman who is two women
will keep pressed flowers,
fossil cake, a motel key.
The neuter angel, glorying at the womb
of Eden, will press a gold ring
on her hand. One will stay
in the dying forest, and one
will set forth, and they
shall be apart forever.

The Mother of Yeast

Where is the mother of dreams?
I have shaken all I can from bushes,
from running, running, two feet
behind the loose arc of my senses.

The Song for Two Mouths is over,
mother, have I drunk my fill
with the grazers of algae and clover?
The windgrass hardens to braille.

Where are my hands going,
tipped by dead stars? The least
stone stirs in the shade, mother of homing
birds, widow of yeast.

The young ones dance in my shadow.
My wrist is a snarl of blue veins.
So I have dressed a bed for the mother
of memory, the child of pain.

How the Hand Became a Glove

How long does the pillow hold
    the shape of two heads?
When does the hand become
    a glove of skin?
Why does the clothing rise
    from abandon
and assume the street?
    The clock slows, but who
is there when the hands loosen
    and the face goes blank?
The stirred pool clarifies
    and in the flowerbeds
Spring and Winter lie so close
    who will tell why the wind
goes bitter one moment
    and moistly urges the next?
The eye picks the rose,
    which is the body in delight,
but who will tell us why
    its fire is frozen?

To the Chairperson of the *Sonnets*

In my Newtonian youth, love songs
hung sweet spittle from my chin.
The green world drew up
into two vast prominences:
man woman man woman
plus and minusing in my bonehead math.
Why the scoutleader left town
in the middle of the night
was as arcane to me
as the luminosity behind
the Horsehead Nebula.
The world stripped down
to its final face, and fire leaped
between cathode and anode,
groin hair swirled, iron filings
around magnetic flow.

Later, in my Einsteinian days,
someone wore my blue jeans on the town.
Lambency haloed the jockstraps
in the dark lockers.
Lines turned in certain poems
and showed their bottoms.
Space was dense with Pulsars,
quasars, lefthanded mesons,
the "strange" particles.
I had to look twice
at whatever I held in my hand.

Dear Chairperson of the *Sonnets*,
were you, or where were you, bearded?
Where do you lay your sleeping head, my love,
at which end of the spectrum?

Looking Both Ways before Crossing

1.

On a day when smoke lies down in alleys,
when a football skitters from behind the parish house,
when a faint bitterness in wines and ciders
curls a moment at the back of the tongue,
I find myself again
an unfrocked minister of change,
looking both ways before crossing.

I set out for the instant,
telling the wind to stop in the trees.
But leaf fires leap into the ash and air,
or sing back along the limb
where the sun picks for its eye
one drop on a leaf.

I am more leaf than tree.
Wind moves its wave forms through my flesh,
time falls from the back of mirrors,
where, through my eyes,
I see the child and skull.

2.

How easy to see an old town as a ship,
with a bow wave of junked cars and chickencoops
plowing with a full spread of elm through grain.
Young men are swimming for their lives,
while their elders become their own potatoes,
holding their thick, broken hands
in the stained light of the church.

Outside, the corn rasps,
black and venereal,
rising from the bones of planters.
What earth can I leave
that does not take me back
under the harsh corn?

3.

Who named me tenant of change?
Why must I chronicle the last places?
Lost riverbeds, closing under willows,
broken wings of kites,
glints of transits
across the valley.

The old hotel shrinks in a desert of parking meters.
What can it say:
drummers, revivalists swollen like a tent,
horse traders?
No, they're tying off the tubes in the basement,
the plumbing has hot flashes,
the walls strip down their paint.
The shaker slows,
and the barkeep fades into the mirror.

4.

I am old enough to be my own father,
and yet the green tongue of spring
stirs me like a child.
In the first yeast of April
I rise to the taut blue of kites,
leaned out over the heeling town.
In the young faces of women,

beauty turns to me
like sudden flowers.
Why must I be father and son,
hating and loving across years?
I want to take my own hand,
and in a still place in the wind,
be what I have become.

Section Three
Everyone Born in 1926

Part I.

Keeping Out of Trouble
for Robert Huff

I've tried to keep out of trouble,
but I'm always falling through women,
untidy bitches with ceramic earlobes.
They smell a brilliant failure on me.
I run out of classrooms, chalky,
my face frozen, and close my office door
on the last, shaken fist of poetry.
Trying to fly, my armpits creaking,
I feel them weight my cuffs, dying,
giving birth, wanting to be read aloud.

Someone was smoking who shouldn't,
the dean squeaks on the telephone.
He shakes your hand as though analyzing
for urine, semen or liberalism.
I hit him with a hard lyric,
and he didn't even wince.

I try not to drink, but the bottle
bows to my fist. My brain fizzes
and makes lights. My nights
are told to me as strange prose
on dry, throbbing afternoons.

I hear the red phone ringing
in the chancelleries of the spirit.
I hear the sift of calcium,

choking the back alley
where all the joints are closing.
I hear the bad music of the needle.

There is no one to send for.
I must be suffered out like a bad hand.

The Cutting Edge

The air rusts upstate. Hills
soar in bronze. Autumn.
We are judged too soon:
the courtly, the moderate, down,
thumbed from the same ripe peach.

You can't see blood against leaves.
October smokes with blood.
Time of the cutting edge.
The gamebag bleeds, the creel.
Gutters run red.

A woman is dying in a room
full of Winslow Homers.
You can see through her.
Autumn has needed her color.
The sea milks in her breast.

In fall, the earth is shorn.
Trees sink in a red splash.
Corn is pared behind the ears.
The hill flares once, then browns.
Ready for the white seeding.

What are you doing on your knees?
The last loving in the grass
before your separate cars turn
their cold butts on one another
and gravel off into the fall.

The green current has failed!
Sap flushes down the trees!

The grape vines fall on their knees!
White explosions rock the greenhouse!
The burner nourishes its electric groin!

I hold my hand in sunlight.
It has gestured forty years.
Each pore is a scar.
The palm is still hot and sexy.
It reaches in the yolk of fall.

YADDO, 1964

Saying the Wind

I've said so much about the wind
it leans in my room like gravity.
I beat to port, holding eggs down,
catching toast by its coarse wing.
All this wind! Outside, the poplars
show their heels. The fluid currency
of undergrowth bucks and bridles.

Once you've made your metaphor,
you lie with it. I kiss your flanks
in a flume of sheets. Your kiss blows
through my head until its halls ache,
family portraits stretch like kites
over the idiot tongue of the carpet.

But this is wind, the alterer,
the signal for the change of face,
the hands no longer meaning
what they touch, the new shift
as love wears down in lax coils.
The wind freshens, turns, aligns. . . .

In 1936, I tied
two sticks into a shaky cross,
diamond-strung its split ends,
flour-pasted wrapping paper,
hung old socks, ties, shirt-strips
under, bridled, strung it, flew it
over powerlines, above town,

pulling, the fear, the need to let go
against it, watch it leaf down,
wind slack in the hands, again.
On the green hill, above the town,
level river gusting on my spine,
I held, I held against the wind.

Wheel of Saturday

The deep wells are drying in Martinsville, Indiana.
Hard water coughs in the pumps.
Once, hills rained to the touch,
millwheels rocked with brown velocity.
Lovers, parked under shale cliffs,
swam uneasily within each other,
hearing the earth shift liquidly
under the crickets of the hill.

I tried to be a stone that ran, then.
Tides swept in me between unknown horizons.
I spun in a whirlpool
around the Saturday square; girls turned
in pairs between farmers, bibbed in blue armor
awaiting their curled wives.

Often I thought I was drowning,
the waters ran so steeply through me.
We all turned neon, circling
the red cuspidor of the courthouse
June Saturday nights.
Now the wells run dry, and twenty years
lime my bones.

Sometimes, in the deepest place,
I hear water turning
the dead wheel of Saturday.

I will not be with you
my skin is coarse as rind
my hair disperses north
a thin cirrus trails my lips, singing
songs that must be cracked like an old walnut
dry and brown as the thorn's fruit

Eat, at the thorn's peril

What Do You Do when It's Spring?

What do you do when it's spring?
I mean what do you do when it's really green
not just in the private parts of the links
but even between the rusting tracks
where the dead train slipped under the fence
into the dead factory?
                              What would you tell
your wife if you woke with a green thumb
and everything you touched turned to grass?
And you still owed six payments on winter?

What would you do with a bird
so small it could swim in and out
through the bars of its song?

What do you say when you can't find your camera
and miss something beautiful, your neighbor's wife
opening at the seams, or the march
of the red tricycles on the fire station,
or the pedlar who is not running a survey
in your neighborhood?

What would you say if the garbage man
cast off his mask of orange and red
butcher's paper and danced between your eyes
the dance of a person becoming himself?
Or if the meter man had a name?
Or if the milkman led up your green driveway
a buxom cow, spraying sweet milk and clover,
wearing a milking machine like curlers
on her horns?

Or if the mailman took root in your box,
shedding green news, and mailing himself
over and over again, into the sprinkling evening?

What do you do when you feel
that the Great God Ampersand links flowers and ceramics,
table salt and Triton, or rocks like a treble clef
beneath the rusted swing and slide?

I mean before schools and jails open.
I mean before the paper knocks at the railing.
I mean before the rose vine loses its legs.

What do you do when you're born?

Looking Up and Down

For days, I never look up or down,
tracing a map of small horizons:
house, office, liquor store,
turning my eyes from face to face,
page to street sign,
feeding the meters.

But miles inland,
streets take the shape of the shoreline.
Whole suburbs dodge the granite head.

Feeling this,
I begin to raise my head
to the honking intersections of geese.
And I begin to lower my eyes
to the Indian trails,
the worn paths of animals
coming to water and salt.

And trolls in the subway earth,
and angels,
making their final approach.

Taking My Medicine

Things floating in and out of my nose
ask me to remember fever, call out
the white troops of the blood
to swell around bad behavior.
I sneeze all I know about germs
into a language course of Kleenex,
full of glottal stops and clicks
that suffer in translation.

My brain splits along dotted lines
to think alongside my sinuses.
I exchange handedness,
go on a night shift of stuttering.
Two suns try to rise in my cheeks.

I float in and out of my nose,
a topological case study,
all one steadily incensed surface.
I don't know which nose is blowing:
the white inner Moby,
or the red, stentorian vizard
mapping its delta of wines;
but both the great sail of a submarine,
saying that atmosphere tests have resumed,
saying the sea's about had it with garbage.

The druggist who failed Urology
told me to drink this straight down
on *either* side of my stomach,
and I'd find my vision would single,
that stethoscopes would vine from his ears,
my brain would put its heads together,

that his nurse would lie back like forceps,
that my eyes would turn around frontwards
as guaranteed by the label.

On Saturday, feeling myself again,
a ribbon clerk at the desk
where the typewriter shook my hand,
I demanded my money back.

Ode to the Smith and Wesson Revolver

I knew your neighborhood when I was young,
across the tracks in "Bucktown."
I didn't know whether the blacks were poor,
or the poor were black,
but when you shone it was the same.
You hung at many strong men's thighs,
cruelty's pudenda.

Although the major hired you when he broke the strike,
socially, you were impossible.
You watched his daughter's wedding gifts,
brighter than the toasters,
but you cut no cake with them.

I thought I had outgrown my need for you,
getting the wife and kids,
an office door that named me,
but tonight I take you out.
Down this street, televisions look at one another
like a row of prison guards.
They say a red button can end the world,
a red telephone can save it.
The man between shakes with sexual desire.
But here we are alone.
We kiss at last.

Asking Directions in California

1.

I'm a stranger here myself, she said.
There's a banquet of streets
and I'm on a diet of discovery.
Hand over hand, I'm hauling myself in
through patience and a long memory.
I'm an uneasy tenant, gathering
mirror pieces from broken compacts
until in and out walk together.
One day at a time, one street
at a time. One of these nights
my cat won't come back.
Then I'll tell you where I am.
You can take it from there.

2.

Farflung, diffuse, unstable,
hidden behind the dead ends of swamps,
shut off by riots and hoses,
diving under channels and coming up roses,
following mail trucks to the morgue,
known by the deaf and dumb,
recently parachuted Armenians,
and drunks, who can't find their way
out of a bottleneck, models
with their heads up their hat boxes. . . .

3.

The women in our family, he said,
have always been artistically inclined.
We make strange maps

where it's always downhill.
You've plenty of gas, your oil's up,
but there's salt on your tail pipe.
You were weaned on a snowball, too.
Here, if you spit,
up yawns a national park, bears,
beer cans, bicycle paths,
and likelihood, a key word,
of being trampled by a frosted baseball team.
This is the way.
Drink Fornical, always bear right,
and you've got it.
Any end to a means,
there's a state flower for you.

4.

I'm a stranger self than here.
You can't miss it.

Just Driving Around

1.

In early August,
the corn comes up over the car
on the back roads.
The only road to anywhere
sometimes is blocked by a great mower,
the driver's neck red as a stoplight.
You stop for gas,
and your grandfather, looking freshly
resurrected for the occasion,
winds up the old pump as if it were
the wellspring of the earth itself.
You boil in the stool like a radiator.

But no, the place is closed.
You stop to take a leak in the corn,
back in that green and yellow,
creaking and rubbing,
heavy-bagged and plumed granary.
Too much!
Too easy to root in and grow something.
You home in to the car antenna,
slowly,
hoping the radio will have been invented.

2.

In those grain elevators,
high and windowless, the sun dreams
with one eye open.
Driving those states you can't see
your way clear of for days, you come on them,
blocking up from the horizon,

secretive as vaults, and reliable
as mortgages.
                    Where I come from,
the barns are so inattentive, so shambling,
they must be held up
by an Indian treaty or a Mail Pouch sign,
saying: those old men who cursed
the cows home have shot their wads
into the bushes for the last time.
They painfully climbed their grandchildren's spinet,
and sat down in an oval frame,
looking as though they needed to spit.

But the grain elevator hums,
down where you can feel it,
that all the long rows end here,
where the closed eye has plans
for us heavy eaters.

O the Protestant loaf,
that can be squeezed fist-size,
is torn by meat paste and mustard,
sent in a little black coffin
to the granary,
in the cathedral towns
of Kansas and Nebraska.

The Sleepwalker

Someone I sleep with rises,
walks down a hall
in dark thick as held breath.
He feels down the stairs,
eases the latch into the street.
Wind lights swing,
and stars arch a vague spine.

There he begins to form.
His face struggles out of flesh,
and his name hardens his tongue.
Small creatures in holes,
tunnels, in the thatch of weeds,
lift their ears in his fingertips,
and his palms breathe.

it is one night given
Around him, the houses open
in his eyes, doors, walls,
blankets and sheets.
He enters all dreams at once:
a king for the mailed prince,
a dead brother forgiving,
falling back in blood
for those who sleep with weapons.
His kiss cools on new breasts,
and children turn and turn
in the fur of their dreams.

On a curled country road
where the field shakes loose,
where the shack wood spirals from paint,

a billboard peels its decades;
each bright, accessible image
flowers, sickens and falls
back through the wars, the depressions,
until the screen stutters black.
Then, in the boards, the whorls
contract, drawing the wood back
into boles, into trees, into seeds.

all things yield their names
When someone I sleep with walks
into dreams that dream us,
become us when we lay down our watches,
our wallets; when someone
I walk with sleeps, all things
spin dark, and sigh loose the light
we close into our lives.

He turns, the dawn vague on his face,
to climb up to waking.
The clock is a spiral nebula,
its siren begins to tremble.
He climbs down into my sleep.

I know I won't remember again,
as I strap on my names. No wake
of dreams will follow me out.
I will drive into the billboards
I have chosen to live for.

Part II.

Some Martial Thoughts

"Things are rough all over,"
we said as soldiers.
To think we fought Japan for apple pie,
Korea for the United Nations,
and the Viet Cong for a debate topic.
The way it's going, my sons will fight China
for abstract expressionism.

Our Texas generals demand so much love.
Gladly, our students cover their typewriters,
march into the television screen.
Only the makeup is real,
the blood real,
those children are really frightened
as smoke eats their village.
The rioters know how to face the camera.

The D.A.R. counts our rings.
Grosse Pointe, Michigan, listed several degrees
of "swarthiness" for their restricted tracts.
The American Legion goosed Chicago,
later doubted the patriotism
of the Campfire Girls. (Would it were so.)
There is no army against these things.
You can burn your birth certificate
and go on living. They have copies.

In 1918, my father was gassed.
I must ask him sometime what he coughs for.

Gloss

from Gen. Leslie R. Groves'
*Now It Can Be Told: The Story
of the Manhattan Project*

1.
"Whatever you may
accomplish,
you will incur the everlasting
enmity
of the entire Northwest
if you harm a single
scale
on a single salmon."

At Hanford,
the Columbia River
cooled the reactors.
Asphalt was poured to protect
the typists' heels.
Morale was high
in the motor pool.

At Los Alamos, General Groves
bought a boys' boarding school
whose teachers were serving elsewhere.
Its owners were happy to sell out
"and close down for the duration—
and, as it turned out, forever."

Hiroshima
Nagasaki
no scales injured
except a few goldfish
101,000 dead
128,000 injured

more or less for the duration,
and, as it turned out,
forever.

Forever it turns out
the target must be large enough
to contain the anger.
Nothing to be learned
from a hole.
Some cities were too small,
others already burning.
Kyoto had culture.

Hiroshima had everything
including American P O W's.

    2.

"Not one was hired
or kept on who had been convicted of rape,

arson,

or narcotics charges.
Such people were felt to be
unreliable
because of their demonstrated weakness
in moral fiber
and their liability to blackmail."

What's a little rape, General?
It shows a crude affection,
something to be learned from a hole,
no scales injured,
cools down those reactors
in the typists' heels.

And arson is really too much.

No weak fiber
in the blackmail
of the Bomb.

All our teachers were serving elsewhere.

    3.
Truman thought long into the night.
General Groves thought long into the night.
The Pentagon thought five ways from the middle.

There was uncertainty about the location
of Heisenberg.

Otto Hahn had "contemplated suicide
when he first saw
the full potentialities of his discovery....
After bracing himself
with alcoholic stimulants
he became calmer...."

General Groves: "I personally thought of Blondin
crossing Niagara Falls on his tightrope...."

Teller was pregnant.

"As General Eisenhower put it, 'I have so many things
to deal with that it puts an undue burden on me to be
given any secret information, as I am then forced to
think
constantly about
what
is secret
and what
is not.'"

The Dead Soldier

Now his body is a uniform.

All the colors have bled
from the gray flag of his face.

He was badly led to this sprawl,
whether by Ike or Priam.

The curly burst to the summer street.
The pain in the groin from the teasing girl.
The pint passed behind the stands.
His being!
The unblessed seeds of his dead children.

He was badly taught to speak out his throat,
in our bad silence.

All his leaders follow
where his torn body points down.

Now his body is a uniform.

Which End of the Stick?

Is it a fire in the head
on top of an ice column,
or a black box, riding a rich,
plundering animal? What chooses,
and what gets on with it?

Those who thump their books,
blueprint-eyed, are they never
drunk and disorderly at think tank
office parties, are they never
vague, ruminating mouths,
venturing a testament of belches?

And you who magistrate a few inches of skin,
crawling in and out of each other
on bended knee, what nose will you follow
when the old brain rinds,
when the scent trails blow away?

Remember those whose eyes light up
just short of madness, the True Way
burning a wire in their brain.
Their faces blazon on store fronts.
Their voices roar from sound trucks.
Great crowds, their countries on their backs,
have fled down Lombardy grace of roads
until the wire burned out at Berchtesgaden.

Then came the millions of Ikes,
with no lights on anywhere

in those dark, rented heads:
a single orgasm of national purpose.

In the street you thought you knew,
out stretches the ebony nightstick
to put the law on you.

Guns

Surely the day will come
when they will bring in the guns to the armory
and be given an acre and seeds
by the old sergeant with frank tears.
In Quincy, they will burn them in the vacant lot,
where the feed store failed, you remember,
and the bulldozers coming in the morning.
Children in arms, and the drunks let out
among the parishioners.
And out near the ore fills, where the freshets ran brown,
Billy Joe Smith, the harelip cousin,
will tamp down the sour dirt over his squirrel rifle.
What will grow there? A cordite daisy,
a squirrel arching his leg over it.
All the animals back, like cats,
to be shooed out of the privies.

Remember, then, in your canines, in your
trigger fingers, in the blood of your temples,
the belts of blue cartridges, Bofors pocking
the Stuka sky, John Wayne searching for something
in his chaps, sorry, it's gone. His grandchildren
will have to look it up in Webster's.
It starts with G, like God.

The Closing of the Victory Bar and Grill

for Richard Hugo

Did we go down in flames after all,
the fuses set short over Ploesti?
Are the mothers grandmothers,
knitting gold stars to wear in their eyes?

I feel a stiffness when I climb down
into my life.
I toss back the last one several times.
Something fabulous is coming up.

When one is a veteran of World War Two
he is likely to have several eyes,
each replaying outrages and illusions:
          the square needle in the left ball,
          the short-arm in helmet liners and raincoats,
          and in the guardroom,
          a crystal ball of VD kits
          for the last virgin to bear arms.
          He will sit in a Biloxi bar,
          looking dangerous, clutching his VD kit,
          trying to pierce a waitress
          with his eyes.
                    Later, he will offer
          the condoms, huge with breath,
          to the vagaries of air,
          where the swollen dream,
          entering the movie house fan,
          dies of applause.

You are thinking this is a long poem.
It was a long war,
and the Victory Bar and Grill

is here to testify that a drinking veteran
dreams a long gullet. He listens close,
hearing what's coming and going,
explosions behind his eyes,
the whip of blood.
If you sing through this gullet,
it takes a while
to come out fabulous.

The sun strikes amber through your beer,
and in its spotlight you see
a product of know-how:
a miniaturized Belsen, with little people
marching, the tower lights
twisted in the wire.
A plume of smoke from your cigarette.
So beautifully preserved,
you don't know whether to laugh or cry.
The skin lampshades, the holy cross
drooping its corners, gold teeth
rattling in the collection plate. . . .

We were lost in that war
and live on the other side of life
with the others that blew up,
where the joyless are gently restrained,
no causes to die for,
where the powerless grow steadily beautiful,
where we tell poems
about the underside of grass.

Now the Victory Bar and Grill is closing.
The short snorter, the picture
of the squadron, flow

to the archives on the combers of this poem.
And we are veterans among you
as the neon darkens,
as the uniforms march under strange banners.

One last beer to that old bitch, World War Two,
and her slant-eyed daughter.

The Bearers of My Name

One was a crane operator,
given to beer, bowling and small pranks.
Soon he will climb into his gold watch
and roll down to St. Augustine.
I operate cranes,
long waders of the riffled lake,
wanting to know and right now
what's swimming under all those mirrors.
And one was the hangman at Nuremberg.

One did not pay for car repairs.
Somewhere in the caverns
of socket wrenches and grease racks,
a pleasant voice, strained down to a wire,
asks me to stand account
in the flesh of my names.
And one was the hangman at Nuremberg.

One swam the butterfly, a difficult stroke,
looking up like a seal
from the gray waves of the sports page.
I do not shout for eggs at morning,
but wings, Where are my wings?
But find too often
closets hanging the years,
frayed knees of advancement,
lapels tugged wide by advice.
No wings,
from the first goldpinned diaper
to the gray despondent cocoons of profession.
A shimmering blackness where the faces should be!
And one was the hangman at Nuremberg.

Feeling Cross Hairs Bristle . . .

Feeling cross hairs bristle
on the back of my neck,
I swing around to nothing,
though one doorway held,
I thought, a deeper night.
I climbed those stairs,
one flight, three, five,
all those sad storeys,
cat corners, food air,
dim watts at landings.
　　To one, this door
is a fingerprint: key scratches,
toe marks, a crayon scrawl.
Inside, not much, journalists,
no swastikas, gun magazines.
A few good bad prints, records.
African Genesis open on the couch.
Clean, scattered, bachelor.
　　Black jackbooted, hard-on,
face half powdered,
half crewcut brutal, I stand
pointing a throbbing gun
at the pointing mirror.
　　Dear, I'm home.

The Unexpected Light

When we hold someone close, does a face
kiss a face, or does a wallet slide
into a purse, ID's tenderly flattened
against ID's?

       If the light goes on
unexpectedly, a bloom of lightning, perhaps,
do we see skin containers, with hair
here and there, and no features?
Vague indentations at the smooth end,
one with a hole, and one with a nailless,
probing finger?

       And the literature
which is squeezed out of the action,
does it cry out like those creatures
that flopped out of steaming, primordial soup
and lined up to be sent off into reptiles
and animals, birds, the chitinous armor of insects?

Do the faces in the wallets and purses,
with particular eyes and smile cuts, caught
in the garden at 334 West Appleton
on August 9, 1968, in a shadowed burst
of radiation, say that they will love forever?

The Day Shall Be Known for Foxes

The day shall be known for foxes.
Where the fisher straightens and curves
the bloody nail of his arm
over streams burly with granite,
the nights shall dream with owls.

The night shall dream with owls.
As lovers see in the dark
that fish swim up the stream
they become as they love in bed,
the summer forgotten for flowers.

The summer forgotten for flowers,
where the rainbow thrashes to silence,
and the fisher drifts down the river,
water filling his footsteps,
the winter remembered for hunters.

The winter remembered for hunters,
where the fox sits grinning near hutches,
but ministries burn in the capitol,
missiles straighten and curve
when the earth spins down into silence.

When the earth spins down into silence,
the day shall be known for foxes,
the night shall dream with owls,
the summer forgotten for flowers,
the winter remembered for hunters.

Three Mornings in September

1. 1936
I wake in my father's house.
Autumn smokes from the earth
as the clock gathers itself, as the sun
shoulders up from the river.
My dog lifts his ears at a neighborly bark,
scrabbles off through the arbor.
The Concords swell, the apples fall
in light wind. Cows swing heavily.

The first shadow thickens on the wall.
Now the sun strikes through the window,
the blind cracked like a blueprint,
through the web-woven barn window
to the searing edge of the scythe.
The oak leans out of its shadow
and silently bursts into flame.
My father tries to cough up the war
in the shallow trench of his sleep.
I tie on my sneakers, drift out
to run awhile with the hounds.

2. 1946
I wake in my father's house.
Autumn coils in the roots
of trees still breathing night.
I know some night will stay
along the vines. Some night will take
the birds, shrill in the oak,
until, as if a north wind whistled,
they will rise in one black cloud
to rain down on a far horizon.

I know that color builds along the ridge,
copper, brass, the bronze pears,
until, like a bomb in Berlin rubble,
a hard leveling of black and white.

An army has taken the town.
Uniforms die in the closets,
with shoulder patches, stripes and ribbons
already turning to Greek.
A far sun lifts from my tan,
old commands ease from my muscles.
The earth aches for the harvest
in the first full year of peace.

3. 1956

I wake in my father's house,
a veteran of thirty tans, hanging
like uniforms in dark closets,
as I march up to the front
of the war which burns in the trees.
Outside an unanswered bark bites on the wind.
My children whisper like hoarse leaves,
eager to run with the hounds
where color gathers on the ridge.

My wife turns from her sleep
the full harvest of her body.
We pull the quilt, bright as fall leaves,
up to the edge of sleep.
We are between wars again.
Snow sends its first, white scouts
into the dreaming valley.
I send this prayer out into the light.
May children wake, in ten years' time,
on the full brink of harvest,
safe in their father's house.

Part III.

Getting Up Too Early on Sunday Morning

1.

What do I want this morning that's good for me?
I've used up my old effects,
now it's time for a new cause.
Stand up and be counted,
or lie down and be counted out.
Shall I attack prejudice where it lives?
Where are my black brothers?
I know a black thing or two about brothers.
Walking the middle of the road
can get you killed two ways.

Shall I live in the past?
Refuse to move out of a condemned tree?
Causes blacken the earth like passenger pigeons.
Look at leaders, pipsqueakers, papsuckers,
popepsychers, poopseekers, popsayers,
potseers, for and against, for and against,
and all in uniform: khakis and boots,
levis and sandals, collars and crosses,
all doing something with their hair,
tonsure, straggle, crew and iron.

2.

On Sunday morning, the Christ radio
swims on every channel, covered
with grease for cold, the hard crossing.
The uvula tremors with scripture;

wherever the finger drops
an oracle vibrates text and consequence
through the dial, on bandspread, between the tubes,
a great, white aura of faith
through comic living room.

Now it will be seen that we must take
the minister's hand, stretched out across AM
through the empty bankbooks of raped strip mines,
over the hungover tenth vice-president,
over the used-car lots (weeds, ten junkers and neon),
over the cities planned like a shotgun blast
for the mind death of infants,
over the publishing house with its poem-eating computer,
over the rotting grain and the starving child,
over the pistol cocked like a penis
at the thigh of the Statue of Liberty. . . .
Inside the plastic box, small lightning
dreams in ozone. Before the world comes back,
pass the plate.

Kill to Eat

In the green, strange eyes of lions
we turn to meat
as though the gray tusks of their paws
swung us through Chicago slaughterhouses.

Being considered impersonally
by a sleepy brown explosion.

The oldest profession,
and the ethics
lying somewhere in the scraps and bones.

But there is some beauty
in serving the heavy-bellied swing through grass,
a long history, mostly red.
But in the eyes of generals, sheriffs
and certain women,
one sees the wars, the prisons, the suburbs,
the crickets of typewriters,
strange oaths before the flag,
condoms and jellies laid out neatly,
and the honorable napalm.
Appetite,
and in a country where no one need go hungry.

Three Herons, Three Rooms, Three Eyes

1.

The first heron climbs down
his leg ladder into
his white breast.
The sun ponders an inflamed navel.

The second trails the wind
of his lost brother,
the dark bird under the wing.
The puckering windlass
in the tidepool
pulls in the star meshes.

The third heron is the white zigzag
at my eye's corner, the gill wound,
the one scar of Eden.
All the herons of sunlight
break in the water.

2.

"This is the room of endless desire:
wall plaques of Sandra,
mounted trophies, lighted cases
full of exploded views
of your organs.

"This is the room of endless belief.
Placards shout in the trees.
The clock swings its heavy sword.
You cast a cracked glove of skin
before the mirrors.

"This is the room of death.
A frontier office in Eastern Europe.
An official examines your papers,
checks a list. The guard
straightens at the door."

      3.

One eye knows compact women
dressed in immense sexuality
or a long green forest
where birds flash their needles.

One eye sees through the mask
of flesh, through embryos,
primitive bargains struck
with functionaries, the full halltree
of motherhood, the rusted handshake.

One eye sleeps
and dreams all other eyes.

Everyone Born in 1926

Everyone born in 1926
won't live to regret it,
knows the Black Widow Spider
eats her mate,
has a red hourglass on her belly.

Everyone born then
will die of a long illness
caught in natural childbirth
and prolonged nursing.

Everyone so born
goes down with all hands,
singing *nearer my God to Thee*,
knowing what the other hands are doing,
caressing the Woman Who Isn't There
in the woman who *is* there.

Everyone born in 1926
looks through a dead fifth
like the Learn'd Astronomer,
at the Little Sperm Who Could,
into the House of Usher.

Everyone born that year
walks through himself on the way
out of one face into another,
through the revolving stairs,
to draw new lightning on his face.

Everyone named
left something behind:

his tongue in a brass retort,
his aria in a fence cat,
his nails in a grease trap,
his eyes in a glass case,
his scrotum in a Jock Museum.

Everyone born in 1926
marches up and down
in front of the Lost Cause,
carrying a placard edged in black,
in a storm of torn mortgages,
following his windsock,
sending his suit to vote,
starting divorce proceedings
against his widow.

J. B. Woods' Son, John

Remember, it was John Woods who told you
    in April the garden would leap up
        like a brown cat, spin twice,
    and come down bristling green
with news from the tail.

Jefferson Blount Woods' son John
    thought he knew every riff
        of black Ecclesiastes
    and the cast in the eye
of walletsized, handtinted holyghosts.

Stand beside me, Professor Woods, let's see
    if you've grown an inch
        since you gathered up your roots
    like hair spats and came down
in the compost of the next county.

It was Woodsy-boy and no almanac
    who shivered all seventeen while the girls
        went to dress for the dignity
    of the Hill Top Motel
and never came back, too bad and thank God.

It was J. Warren Woods who ran
    until he was red and drank
        until he was white and blew
    until he was blue in the face
some mad tale of Nutter's Hill and kites.

The line waiting for grades can peel off.
    The line wanting advice can shuffle itself.

Those wanting sugar tits can suck,
and pre-post neurotic women
can carry off their couches on their backs.

It's my home stand, people, I'm holding sway.
I know my own mind or whatever
wills green ears in the shrubbery.
Come in and howdy the top part
because the roots have a one-way to the elements.

You had your chance to ring my nose,
bell my tail and bug my sperm,
brand the neck of my laundry
and cauterize the frank blood
of my stare. Johnny was here but he left.

3,500 Lb. Clock

In the garage, a black Chevrolet
sits and keeps good time.
The carburetors sniff at the gas tank,
and the distributor
is a dead merry-go-round.
It's waiting to take me to the hospital
to be born.

Look at those crutches doing the two-step!
They almost make my bones snap
in sympathy.

The piano follows me around,
arching its back, purring.
Nice pussy, such white teeth.

Dust flies up the sunshaft.
Night drips in the room under the sink.
The watercloset fills and empties and fills.

There's a beard in the closet
and an old crewcut.
I think I'll step in and hang.

Affection for Machinery

1.

:affection for machinery,
    simple straight razors
called *Tuesday*, *Wednesday*, *Friday*,
    stropped sickle-thin.
Heavy fixtures in the men's room
    of La Salle Street Station:
"ascending the throne, he regally
    tore off three feet of paper."

The massive oiled flanks
    of the steam locomotive
in Greenfield Village.
    The old cars, each with a pan
to catch incontinence.
        Poor old
    fathers, wetting yourselves,
commode rust staining
    your pure white beards.

2.

How clearly a spoon must think of its duties.
It hoists your soup and sings of coupons in a clear treble.
It shakes off your saliva
and lies down in the drawer with its brothers and sisters,
amid some danger in that black alley
with those con knivers and mutton forkers.

Poor fist cup, water leaks from every knuckle.
If you ever fill that mouth up there,
it all drains out, now and later.

Poor brain, with so many trains out in the midwest,
rushing toward stalled school buses, when you sleep,
your dreams are the fat sparks from boiling soup.

The spoon dreams
like a metal column,
a star throat, a mercury cadenza,
staring into the dense universe with a silver eye.

3.

Three times I have named an old Ford
as it sinks into earth behind the smokehouse
but no name surges it up,
wheels blurring, barking blue smoke.

There must be affection for something
you can drum on with a bottle,
that chased chicken leaves
from red clay roads,
and gurgled later like that woman
you rode to the picnic.

You're down on your knees,
with somber eyes, searching for the road
back to the ore rift.

Lord Henry is lean in his high collar,
but he will row you across
the Detroit River,
if there is a Detroit and a Detroit River
when you become earth.

Poem by Water

Well met beside the attitudes of water,
we spent the day beneath the creaking bridge
that led from cornland into factories.
Beneath our hanging images the fish
were poised between the reeds and smoking slag.
Above our shadows, the green and scorching wind.

Our words of love were shaken in the wind
that broke a wheel of ridges in the water.
Although we called on fire, the belching slag
built its burial mounds beneath the bridge
and, upside down, betrayed the sliding fish
who hoped for parks but entered factories.

We know the fields of corn are factories.
Their smoking tassels tower in the wind.
They spread their lungs beneath the earth as fish
beneath the creek, weaving the sun and water
into grain. Two worlds are one beneath the bridge.
A single sunlight greens the cooling slag.

And when the fire has frozen in the slag,
the glazing residues are factories
of color, glacial masonry, a bridge
of stone through which the umbers wind.
But poisons fatten in the oily water,
the surface thickening with floating fish.

Though we lie down as lovers, not as fish,
we see the steam that rises from the slag.
It is our breath, our heritage of water.
Words of love are lost in factories

where all is knotted, knotted as the wind
that tilts the rasping weeds beneath the bridge.

The corn is loud. It tells another bridge
that links us, one to one; that links the fish
to spawning when rocks lay melting in the wind,
when men had fins and mountains leaped from slag.
I say these worlds are one: the factories
discharging smoke, the corn distilling water;

I say we walk a bridge as old as wind.
O let us enter factories of water,
breathe love on slag, and turn it into fish.

Margin

Farmers have red corduroy necks;
shoulders, the color of new milk.

Their hands are old harness leather,
and their feet are pale and shy.

Because I am all one color,
my dreams are murderers.

Animal

The night is watched by the flooded ear
of the fox, the great animal ear
in angled burrows, in hutch and runnel,
on springing limb, feeding on oak rustle,
on least creak of wind tacking a point
nearer itself. The earth hears! The earth hears!
Each muzzle knows where it is,
where you are and what you intend.

They flash in and out of life, at headlight edge,
in shopping center, across the snow fence
into throughways, entrails cast by cars
fleeing the future. You will see them gnaw loose
from traps, or trapped, pelt the walls of river shanties
with old magazine covers. Caught, too,
on car fenders by dentists with rented fangs,
who, faced all year by carnivorous throats,
revert to man in the hunting season.

Now I stand in the watched night
in a field of sense. The night is known
by the animal of my body: the ten nails,
by eyes set back in bone, the red meat of my tongue,
by testicles drawn in from cold and wolves.
I step from the dead skin of my shoes.
My lost glove melts in leaves. My watch widens,
numbers cast against the stars.

Animal, I call you out from cage,
where you are taught to stink, from bulldog mask,

where you're bred to suffocate,
from chow in deep analysis.
You pour in litters from the earth, then die
to God knows where: a heaven of leaping and scent,
or a night, fallen from its stars.

Section Four
The Ancient Communities

*"Men who share the same rooms,
soldiers or prisoners, develop a strange
alliance as if, having cast off their
armor with their clothing, they
fraternized every evening . . . in the
ancient community of dream and
fatigue."*

Camus, *The Guest*

Part I.

Going to the Field

1.

I knew the corn for its green swords.
Three times my height, it dueled,
creaking woodenly, for the tassels
of the princess. In October, armed
with lath, I cut its brown soldiers down.
The sun sparked on the fallen armor of ice.
Rabbits broke from cover at each step.
Spring, spring, then the shot spun them.
We ate them in their table shapes,
and spat the buckshot from our jaws.

2.

Some day the field will rise
on its green wings, trailing
compost and filaments of root,
and come to you, where you die out
your insurance on a Florida beach,
or in the cold, upstairs bosom
of your children, or the colder
chamber of the state-supported heart.
The army medal, the gold watch,
the testimonial luggage, the letters
from the enemy you won over
or from the woman whom you warmed
will burn into pure elements.

It will come to claim the furrows
in your face, the hands twisted
by killing and planting too many seasons.

    3.

Now all the cycles slow. Like a dream
of slow, drifting clouds, the field
flowers once, yielding
its sweet pleasures. Then you run again,
hewing the enemy, suddenly
brown and brittle in full retreat.
And you will stand there in the white season
until the field takes you under, mulls
out your seed's worth, and casts up stone.

Passing the Eyes of the Old

In spring, the young love lightly
from the loins. Mirrors fill with laughing,
with tan bodies.
                        No place is secret long:
parked car, the last flickering row
of Chaplin revivals, the golf course,
under the Dean's nose.
                        Old eyes watch
from summer porches, not with envy,
knowing the young leaves coarsen,
the ripe worms web the catalpa tree.
Old movies wind through their dark,
when they were californian.
                        The eyes
of the old strike bone, already urging
from their skin as though to leap.
In pain, betrayal, through bars at visiting hours,
wakened by bad sleep, the eyes, the eyes
of the young are already old.
                        In delivery rooms,
by children lost near water, the young begin
to build their faces.
                        On October Saturdays,
the frat house mirrors open, show
the doubled features of the summer laureates,
who remember the winning season,
who drink because they need it.
After the game, they head for home.
Each road is guarded by a drive-in screen.

Later, the sitter gone with her knitting,
the children sleeping out of time,

they sit, in the depression
of their thirties.
            They watch TV, dreaming
before old movies, when the stars were young.

Terrible Is the Child

Terrible is the child
at whose white temple the blue river reels,
whose finger on the leaf is the leaf's fall,
who in the fallen days
runs like firelines in the leaves.

Terrible is the child
for whom maiden aunts will prophesy,
cutthroat of the soft menagerie, careless
in his love and feeding, needing
only skill to kill with love.

Terrible is the child
who perforates the evening with his cries,
who plays at love and war and ownership
and leaves them strewn across the world
for parents to deserve.

Where an Old Hand Has Touched

Do you know an old field,
where clocks turn in barn boards
and nails clot in timbers?
Can you see a tunnel in trees,
and a clearing, far off,
where the sun breaks into leaves?

Wherever an old hand has touched,
you turn a sign to the wall,
for it says *salt* and *gray moss*
and *something is beginning to forget.*

Wherever an old father rocks,
whenever only a bark comes back
from the coon night, what is it
swings the tire behind the shed?

The class reunion tries to keep
the schoolhouse from sinking.
Earth is up to the windows.

Out in the stubble past the diamond,
around, around,
wind turns its blind, dreaming head.

Following the Moon

You must believe
        there is a moon
rising in your fingernails
          and that it rises
from your heart cistern
          from the salt drum
red caul cap of the long surge
          out of the cells

You must believe
        your hands curl
into yellow wall antlers
          Squeeze ten stars
at your knuckles
        still the moon leaps
from the blood plain
          every night of your nights

        Yes you came down
from your father's house
          to the orchard
where limbs bent to the grass
          and took those red hearts
in your palms
        and felt summer
shudder in them
        Though you named them
this for the plate
        these for the ciderpress
the moon opened a stone eye
        and though they
called your name

from the high house
the window closed
a brown weed shook
dry pods in the empty lofts
of the apple trees

The Eye Coin

to wake under coins
                    a moon with a number
the quince of serum
                    hanging from the bedhead
the wire with a button
                    the nurse's plexus
leading from here
                    the long coat sleeve
black, homespun
                    under the coin night
leading to mother
                    mother I am older than you
the long coat arm
                    the weaving peristalsis
leading to night nursing
                    the button wire
ring in you
            in your lovely body
such shuddering alarms
                    we are not dead yet
once more
            we are not dead yet
the warm earth dries
                    as the sea falls
far in the sunfire
                    the great hawks
turn their last circles
                    before blindness
the white coins drop
                    a face, a year
in the dead white house

                            we rent
            when the streams
                            ring up silver
            red remnants
                            bluster their tree shapes
            and veins darken
                            here on this sheet
            in this rented room
                            this leaf body
            the alarm veins
                            the sleeve of birth
            all bodies are rented
                            all houses white
            the coins stare sanely
                            into our eyes

Pore Nightmares

There are men who put white stones
on the eyes of cisterns
for the sound of falling water
loosens their groins.

As water falls, it forgets the shapes
of spume, waterwheel, lake slap,
the whirling diffusion
near the stars.
                    Nearing earth,
it becomes the tear, enters
the widening eye at the bottom
of the cistern. And the men
whose tears have cast salt stones
close the tunnel of their eyes.

And there are women who fear pores,
who dream pore nightmares.
They study the art of lip hiding.
Do my pores show? And rub orange gel
over their head and shouders.
When they look behind them
in the mirror, they wonder if pores
are following them.
                    A stretched pore
is a wrinkle, a stretched wrinkle
is an earth-furrow, where a linen-wrapped
ferrule of bones tries to remember
its great-grandchildren.

Alcohol

for Philip Schultz

We sit down together
    in the house of alcohol.
Rain threatened all afternoon,
    a brown organ over Chicago,
varicose with lightning,
    as we sat reading poems
by the blue light of alcohol.
    The troops are out in the war
against crime, against poverty.
    Their eyes are blinking red
with sober, arterial blood,
    but we have ringed our hands
in the family of alcohol.
    One is on the slope of dreams.
One has invented a lost diction.
    Many have lost the point of their bodies,
but the fire is laid deep
    against the Michigan winter,
here in the warm trades of alcohol.
    The inventor of wineskins
tells the dream that led him
    from the factory in Antwerp.
No light in the East,
    but the urgency of corks
which felt their time had come
    told him *lay down your clipboard*
and found the company of alcohol.
    It is true that the features thicken
as the Family Face rises
    from its genes, that the slobbering
beast in the garage
    may leap like a weapon, but that

was the prophecy of the Book of Alcohol.
    The grape, grain, even the potato
can rise from the slums
    in the epiphany of alcohol.
Come to it if you can,
    on hands and knees, if necessary.

    We have heard of the kingdom of marijuana
from sweet and noble emissaries
    who speak with smoking tongues.
Although they know not our ways,
    we must embrace in this short world,
lest, again and again,
    old Capulet and Montague must pour
their sour cups over the deep graves
    until the world burns like alcohol.

Part II.

When Senses Fled

I am custodian of close things.
Even winter trees have blurred
to leaf, and faces come upon me
suddenly. I am a startled man
to half the town, and half my yard
is blunderland. First, I lost
the violets, then the grass,
and now, the red and wren-white fence.
Farewell, the bright decay of oak,
the crewcut water, the black assizes
of the night. Farewell, the visual.

Today, the wind began to lag
and all its freight of season drained
into the neighbor trees. And all
the smoking, sideburned streets
dropped ashes on the muted playground.
Let lightning slam the screen, I cry,
let neighbors war, a shop of cats
tear metal. O stone me with shouting.
But the grating thunderhead suspends
its buzzing nest beneath my bough.
Farewell, the audible.
                    Touch,
tell me what the world displays
for now I rain behind my eyes.
If you would hurt me, gather close,
for in the last deception, skin,

I must be broken by a kiss.
Love is a cave of scrolls, and I
have thrown away all spectacles.
I roll horizons like a hoop
among the mufflered trees, and see
nerve ends crackling in the dark.
Farewell, the tangible.
                              Inside,
I stand, a coalescent dust.
When I sing, my voices turn
to stone, and where I touch, veins
stand out. When I am alone, the forest
swarms with nakedness, and where
I point, pole stars waltz along
my finger. Look, the fence appears,
then grass. And all my senses step
on naked feet into the garden
to ring, an anvil of the storm,
to name the kneeling animals.

Silage Courage

So clearly the lion
circles the goat in the one man
that the green fringe
is blood-spotted. Flat teeth
ground the watergrass
as the sabermouth dropped.

The same sun rises in the trees
and the rose bobs to the surface
for the lion and the goat
in the same man; and he licks
old chops for the green blood
as it reddens.

Yes, the barley lover can turn
and show boar's teeth,
but next to the night drinker,
the owl-lion, it seems silage courage.

As the tabby feints along the scent,
hanging ten needles, a mouth
of barbs in the same man;
and in the same man,
a hoofed mood grazes,
are we surprised that the President
sleeps with his generals
and sends his wife to the armory,
or that the lover sometimes mouths
the family loaf until it bleeds?

Light behind the Eye

What did I bring home
to the cave mouth?
Old treelimb burning
its red, eyewatering eye
against the night eyes
and saber mouths.
Our shadows danced into gods
on the socket of the cave
in ochers and umbers,
ashes, blood and grease.

This eyebone you dig from marl
should be raised up
over your head, until it takes
the semen of white electricity,
until it shudders
the stone bass of old gods.

Eye

We have eyes out, gyros spinning,
where the sun roars over the horizon.
There great heliotropes wind
                              mill
in gusts of radiation.
                    Below,
the Amazon aches, a silver
scar.
        Eyes out where the moon flag,
stiff with wire
              ripples,
its pale stars open to the wrenching
edge of the galaxy.
                    We dream
            moistly
        beside the phosphor
clock face
while all the world's waters
raise
        vast hackles to the moon's palm.
As we make speech for a wet lip,
            plasms
arc from the sun,
                neutrinos
fall through planets,
                copper sulphate
builds crystal cities
in beakers.
                Now the gas giants
and the white dwarfs
                roar
messianically, and our nightmares

cloud the Petri dishes.
                    Once,
in a steaming poolstrand, a spine
remembered to gather long chains;
          an eye
winked in a dense ganglion;
          a fingerprint
ridged, snowflake of oil;
          an animal throat
tortured out the bark of his name.
          So, the refrigerator
     has grown
wise with beards.
                    Hydrogen and Oxygen
          drip
     past
the worn washer, or flare
                         deep prominences
to the void.
          So,
after its million-year sleep,
          a star eye
opens in a skin face,
                    down
the mirror halls
of Palomar.

The Night of Even Breathing

In this night of even breathing,
I am awake, but through my wife,
my sons, the halls and piano
moves the sound of even breathing.
From the heater, the open eyes
of three guitars, in books
and saved string, the night
of even breathing spins steadily.

The house breathes through its pores,
the attic vents, a slow breath,
deep pulse. Some waters move
a little in the walls, and lightning
turns over dreamily in the meter.

So the town breathes, the trees
lean down a little, the grass heavy.
Only the lovers, the dying
and the bloodhunting owl
make red flowers on a black vine,
the long vine of even breathing.

The Room under the Sink

Silence calls
dark rooms into the light:
the pantry, sour basement, bedrooms
crying out what has happened in them.

From the dust coils
of the refrigerator, the room
under the sink, a silence
enters the body.
Eyes plunge down the tunnels
of the pulse. The scalp twitches,
and ears hear backward
what has happened to everybody.

Soon,
with every human mouth
stoned shut, and every human memory
broken on the wall,
something beautiful will run
through the parks.

But now, close to roots
and large stones rolled insanely
across the land,
something is crying.

What Is Holy?

What is holy and will it come again?
We fall through a comet's tail
    and call that dust Star.
Heat curls to the poles and winks out.
A bright leaf twitches
    and we call it Time.
We blow our small loves
on our frozen hands,
    hands that reach out
past the Magellanic Clouds,
but which now return, trailing
    hoar frost through the orchards.
We stir in ancestral sheets,
hearing the dull artillery
    of the fruit
in the bone rack
of our breasts.

The Doors We Enter

Already the street has flashed, once, twice,
and it is spring.
A green distemper sets our teeth on edge.
In a sweating fury
we shrug out of wool-gathering, and walk through
the garden door
into the season, *and the season doubled in the pool.*
Know that when the bronze shield
rang in the sky, and a plume of birds rose and settled
in the airtree *and the watertree,*
the shield rang and broke in the red afternoon
of the two gardens,
and on one harsh wing the birds leaped down
the horizon wire.
Know that when we walked out that day, the short rains
shocked down the valley,
once, twice, again, each step a seeding in wet
cloisters, under drumtrees,
grassdriver, green igniter, hedgerow urger.
But know each step
stamped a cider boot in the steadily falling,
dogbarked orchard
when we lay down in the bronze glissade of trees,
loving full-length green.
And as our bodies shuddered and gave their fruit,
the shield broke,
the eyes of the pool began to film and close
when the great wooden plow
turned our bodies under, though the seasons spun
as one, in our closed hands.

Why Adam and Eve Came Sadly to Love

Three months into love,
she searches her lover's face.
Outside, a slow northern spring enacts itself.
For a time, sexuality has lit
a pleasant candle in their chalices.
They have the ribald gift.
And for a time, this room is locked
against processionals, the night Pullman
where hands palm business cards.
But summer gathers, empowering the world.
Soon it will knock, soon it will telephone.
First things first, he said, and knelt
between her thighs. But first things
are first things only.

Usually, we fall blindly down our years.
Sometimes when we give our bodies
to another, we feel like faces,
and where we touch becomes an eye.
The eye is blind, but knowing.
But the harder we press together,
the more we feel something push away.

But now, three months into love,
they lie together. Beside them on the bed
sit a man and a woman from time before,
through whose eyes shine
all things we do to one another. "Play,"
they spake as one. "The world rears
at the end of our eyes, arches
a knubbly back under our palms.

But we outlive our pets, and the wild ones
will not stay with us. Play and stroke,
for we leave a fog of breath on this windowglass.
We lay a wreath of oil with our fingertips.
Now we will lie together.
Soon you will be tired.
You will close your lids and then your eyes."

Lying Down with Men and Women

When we came up from water, our eyes
drew to the front of our heads,
and we had faces. When we came up
on our knuckles, we held fruit to our mouths,
and wanted to know the chemistry
of sweetness.
             Then as we walked down
the earth's curve, trees and hills
got in our way, so we moved them
for roads and newsprint and wreckage.

Part of every day, the water mood and the tree mood
rise in our bodies, and we must
lie down a bit to honor our lost
tails and gills.
             When we lie on our backs,
we see so far away we try to give names to light,
like wild dogs we have taught
to lick our hands.
             And when we lie on our faces,
we see too close, the blank wall
at the end of the corridor.
             And so
we lie down with men and women
because we are terrified, and sometimes,
for that reason, we stand up and kill.

The Five Dreams

What are the five dreams of the elders?

Richard, for all his beard, has seen
mist on an autumn pond and hears
water, the color of cognac, rising
and falling in the reeds of the shallows.
He thrusts his fingers through his hair
and each nail glistens with oil.
He knows that water is giving and taking,
and that it will give and take though fists
slam shut, though the high curse
of his name burns on the door plate.

Wayne is backed against a wall of books,
and the fireplace, the *place* of fire,
reddens his forehead. In his nostrils,
two cables of air freeze, and on them
he hangs in the world. He spreads his arms,
one hand the wing of a leather testament;
the other, the one with a dead ring,
seizes a last book of poetry.
The fire eats all shadows but one.

These were two dreams of the elders.

Emily has brushed her hair forever.
Now it is earth, and pours to her feet.
Half moons glint at her fingertips,
and sand drifts from her mouth, her ears,
the corners of her eyes. She is content.
It was prophesied. Her children look in

at the windows, pale as moonlight.
Remember when they gnawed her breasts?
When she is empty, they will press her
in a book, the book of earth.

Mary knows there are dead places in her.
The doctors, well, the doctors are guessing.
Richard's kiss is dead, but we all
shed layers, and when we have been struck
too often, part of us turns to the wall.
She knows, too, that when the last cobs
of snow melt, green incoherence leaps
from eye to eye. And Wayne's ring?
Well, it turned green before it died.
She takes it off. It pings on the parquet.
The ring scar reddens. She feels better.

This is the last dream of the elders.

Each house has a room that's always locked.
This is the room of dreaming. Sometimes
it is a room of water where a huge eye
glares. Sometimes there is a bed
of glacial sheets, slow, slow, and in them
we can see our gill parents. And, praise God,
one night the young of us will lie down together
in a shadow of black hair. And one day
we will return, put down our cases,
pass through the room where the fist
opens, where the earth sifts, where the ring
spins to quiet. Then, we lie down in the milky,
slow sheets, when the door closes
and is a door no longer.

Striking the Earth

As we strike the earth with our bodies,
for we are always falling, and standing up,
and falling again, though you call it dancing,
or walking, or flying, there is the sound of stone
coming to rest in quarries, the last spray of sand,
as we knock on earth's sullen, historical face.

If we are men with such manners, we lie down
on women and hold a heart-length of warm earth.
You will ask me if we have deserved as much,
as men, so long from the mother. Yes,
but some of us would hold that pose forever.
Stones can leave scars on naked backs, remember,
and the backyard tom has a limited voice.

There are times we strike the earth
like coastal rain, thin but steady, when colors
fade from store fronts, and dawn
might as well be dusk, and both night.
The black box on the last page of the rural weekly,
passing of long cars with lights on, and flags,
as though they might become lost in that night
they have been chosen to carry, rain-wet,
with police sanction, to the plain of skulls.
Funereal, we say of that clothing and steady rain,
when we hang our names and flags in a dark closet,
when the priest turns off the lights below,
and the sound of dirt falling reminds us
of rain through leaves, or the world's bedridden breath.

Every few years we need the quick downpour,
like rivers on end, seeing the oak stump

hammering the pilings, the car light shining
at the bottom of deep wells. These are our wars.
Tonight, if you lie and listen to the soughing
rale of your breath, you may understand
why some men take up edged weapons, or stare
at ceilings from red bath water.

There are unique colloids of water and oil,
but white horses pull a box so light
they don't even lather up, so light even the gasses
are colorless. The skin can be read through,
and the book of the eyes slides back,
unread, into the case. The fingerprint rests
a moment on the flower, then sinks into its
dizzying spiral. A spring day can be a room
kept just the way it was when someone lived,
the black wreath blossoming. Though we eat
decay with both hands, the bruise
is the sweetest part of the apple.
Names that burned, that kissed deeply
to the brain stem, that owned the Tartar plain
from the high fur saddles, weather on stones,
coming to rest in quarries.

Index of Titles

Index of First Lines

About the Author

John Woods lives in Portage, Michigan, and teaches at Western Michigan University. The poems in this book were chosen from six previous volumes, printed between 1955 and 1976 by Indiana University Press. His most recent collection, *The Valley of Minor Animals*, appeared in 1982 from Dragon Gate.